KIKI KERAMIDA

Experiences
of a
spiritual
healer

MEGAS SEIRIOS
Publications

KIKI KERAMIDA
EXPERIENCES OF A SPIRITUAL HEALER
1st EDITION 2014

ISBN: 978-960-7350-86-2

This book is published by **Megas Seirios Publications**, founded by the **Servers' Society Spiritual Centre** based in Athens, Greece. To find more information about the mission, works and activities of the Society and/or to place an order, please visit our website:
www.megas-seirios.com

or contact us at:
9, Sarantaporou Street, Athens, Greece, P.O.: 111 44
e-mail: info@megas-seirios.com
Tel.: +30 210 20 15 194
Tel./Fax: +30 210 22 30 864

Translation from Greek: Dimitris Fragogiannis

Cover and book design: Marianna Smyrniotou

This Book is published by the members of Omilos Eksipiretiton (the Servers' Society) as a token of gratitude to Mrs Kiki Keramida for her dedication to the work of spiritual healing.

∽

CONTENTS

PROLOGUE

When I received the first manuscripts of Mrs Kiki Keramida's book, I was pleasantly surprised. I did not know that she had begun writing a book, I only knew that she was considering the issue, wanting to follow the prompts of the Master, who had advised her to write down her personal experiences from spiritual healing. The Master, poet and philosopher Dimitris Kakalidis is the founder of the spiritual centre "Omilos Ekspiretiton (The Servers' Society)". Throughout his entire life, alongside his writings, the Master taught the Society's members proper human relationships, self-knowledge and spiritual principles. As discussed in the following chapters, spiritual healing was also part of his teachings, followed by those who were interested in this vocation.

My acquaintance with Mrs Kiki dates back to 1982, when she first came to the Society. Since then a friendship grew between us which was based mainly on our common interests; our spiritual course, our search for the causes of humanity's problems and our inclination to participate with every possible way in the efforts made by many people to solve these problems. We were both disciples of the Master and often attended his teachings together.

Mrs Kiki showed a particular interest in spiritual healing from the beginning of her discipleship. Because of this, soon she was entrusted with the responsibility of organizing the healing section which had started to operate within the Society under the Master's guidance. From that time she devoted herself completely to this project. She set up the groups of healers, dealt with the monitoring of patients who asked for the help of spiritual healing and she undertook the task of conveying to those who wanted to become healers the teachings she received from the Master as head of the healing section. Her experiences from her contact with patients, from the healings that she and others performed, as well as from her personal course as a spiritual healer were significant, as will become apparent in the following chapters.

At the time that Mrs Kiki gave me the first manuscripts of her book, she seldom came to the Society herself, as she was not in good health. The cancer that had been troubling her for years had metastasised to the bones and she had to take many precautions in accordance with her doctors' instructions. My pleasure at her decision to write the book was naturally accompanied by the wish that, under the circumstances, she had time to finish it. This, however, did not happen, as the state of her health constantly deteriorated and the pace of her writing decreased; as a result the book was not completed. Mrs Kiki finally succumbed to her illness in the beginning of 1997. Shortly before her death, she handed me all of the chapters she had written and asked me to make certain corrections which she could no longer do.

In accordance with her wish, I worked on the texts she had given me, made the necessary corrections without interfering with the spirit of the book and added certain elements in the end for the completion of its meaning and content. I came to the decision that this book should be published because the experiences of a spiritual healer can provide valuable information to those interested in spiritual healing. Her daughter, as well as the other members of the Society's Board, agreed with this decision. Mrs Kiki was one of the main members of our spiritual centre and one of the Master's oldest disciples. Her work as a spiritual healer actively proves the applicability of the teachings she had received from the Master.

Klairi Lykiardopoulou
President of Omilos Eksipiretiton

INTRODUCTION

This book is being written by a patient who for twenty five long years has been battling cancer. I mention cancer in the book's introduction because, as I address in the next chapter, my illness became a motive for me on my quest for spirituality and led me to dedicate myself to learning and practising spiritual healing which I was taught at "Omilos Eksipiretiton" ("The Servers' Society" spiritual centre). This is one of the highest vocations, with a very broad field, and many of its elements still need to be explored before we can say that we know of all the possibilities it has to offer. Nevertheless, my constant and long-time work as a spiritual healer allows me to be certain that

*the knowledge on spiritual healing has progressed suffi-
ciently for the person interested to be able study it up to a
very satisfactory level.*

*Spiritual healing is based on the basic principle that all
beings in the universe are of the nature of the Spirit. This
is what I was taught at the Society and it is also support-
ed by many scholars exploring the nature of the world and
the nature of the human being. Cancer, as in fact all other
diseases, are caused by our conscious or unconscious re-
sistances to this nature, by our needs, our weaknesses,
our ignorance, our limited mind. A precondition for the ef-
fectiveness of spiritual healing is to recognize our spiritual
nature and use this power consciously for the transmuta-
tion of negative aspects to positive, of illness to health.*

*This principle, which has been mentally validated to
me and has been proven daily with the practice of spir-
itual healing, has helped me greatly in coping with my dis-
ease all these years. Since I have not, however, attained
such a level of advancement as to make the pure power
of the Spirit entirely my own consciousness and experi-
ence, thus I cannot always overcome the difficult situa-
tions caused by my illness. I cannot say, for example, that
I do not feel the pain. The pain exists and it is an undeni-
able fact. What I do achieve, though, and what I consider
an important accomplishment, is the acceptance of pain
and of any physical hardship occurring at any particular
moment. This is a significant result – one of the results –*

of my training on spiritual healing. The training, however, of the spiritual healer goes on forever, because it concerns one's spiritual advancement, the broadening of the mind and heart, the course into the Spirit's light. I describe this course, as I experienced it, in the following pages.

Over the fifteen years of my discipleship at the Society, I have received essential elements from its teachings. These differentiated constantly inside me, depending on my ability to understand them each time, and, as time passed, they gradually took their right place in my consciousness helping me to mature all the more. I was helped greatly in this when I undertook the responsibility of the Society's spiritual healing section which led me to the quest for more relevant knowledge as well as the regular practice of the vocation. I do not know for how long my health will allow me to be in the service of spiritual healing but my intention is to make full use of the abilities it has given me, exercising the vocation and passing on my experiences to all those interested in being helped by it or even becoming healers themselves.

In the Servers' Society spiritual healing is practised by the spiritual healers that have received special training. This training increasingly cultivates their ability to recognize the presence of God within everyone and everything and to work on their conscious union with the divine throughout all their functions and, especially, during the healing. They are also trained to recognise that every form of treatment, classical medicine or alternative methods, is in essence spiritual healing since God is "Ubiquitous and all Pervading". They learn to see the healers of all methods as well as the healing agents they use in the same way, recognising that they, too, are of the nature of the Spirit.

The healing section of the Society realises the need to continuously and responsibly inform the public of the way spiritual healing works and of its positive results for all those resorting to its services. Our experience proves that more and more people are genuinely interested in finding new ways of dealing with their problems and receiving help from spiritual healing. The President of the Society, Mrs Klairi Lykiardopoulou, has already written two books on the function and importance of spiritual healing. This book presents in a more detailed way some of the healings that have been performed at the Society in order to help readers better understand the healings described. Our goal is to make the potentials of spiritual healing known with the hope that, in the near future, it will work in collaboration with the doctors at the clinics and hospitals of our country, as is done in other countries, for the more substantial aid of the patients; an aid that will provide for both the body and the soul of the person.

DISEASE: AN INCENTIVE
FOR SPIRITUALITY

The desire to know one's true nature and spiritual state of being is hidden deep within every person. Most of the times, this desire is not realized unless something happens that urges him or her to come in contact with spirituality and become its conscious seeker. The cause that usually creates the need for such a quest is a negative experience, a physical or mental pain, a disruption of the established way of living that reverses one's inner and outer order and disturbs one's balance. Searching then begins for a solution to the problem that arises and gradually comes the affirmation that the only way out of everything, the panacea, is the spiritual course, the road that lies ahead as one senses the existence of the hitherto hidden spiritual side of oneself.

The incentive that gave me the final push towards the path leading to God was my disease along with all of its dramatic aftermath. I had, of course, been given other, smaller urges up to then but I had let them go unnoticed, as my ignorance prevented me from understanding their meaning in time and making proper use of them.

It was the summer of 1972 when I first had to undergo a difficult surgery while experiencing a serious health problem. There was a tumour in my right breast which the doctors, with external palpation alone, had concluded was malignant, recommending the immediate removal of the entire breast. As I had requested of them from the beginning, in consultation with my husband, they immediately made their diagnosis known to me. I wanted to know the whole truth in its every detail – at least I thought I did – no matter how much mental anguish it would cost me. And it really did cost me, as it turned out from the way I reacted upon hearing the truth.

My first and most obvious reaction was a wave of uncontrollable rage and anger towards everyone and everything, mainly, though, towards the doctors monitoring me, and especially the surgeon that made the diagnosis and whose surgery would irreversibly mark my body. No swimming or sunbathing that summer. And I who loved the sea and the sun! I was forced to end my summer vacations at that point and along with me my husband and child, too. Could this be the reason I was experiencing such anger? Of course it wasn't!

Today, looking back on those events with more composure and prudence, I am able to discern with greater clarity the various aspects of the truth and drama they held which I then diligently kept hidden within my unconscious as I could not bear to see it even though I wanted to believe the opposite. I can now discern the fear for the discomforts ahead of me, the fear of death which came as a sure and irreversible conclusion. I remember that the only thing that gave me a small comfort was the thought that "from the moment we come into this world, we all have death inside us."

I withdrew into myself and said nothing of my feelings to anyone. I stubbornly gave in to my emotions and had no desire to delve deeper within for their true cause. I only wondered, as I looked inside myself seeing attributes I never knew existed, how I had become so intolerably egocentric and so indifferent to what other people might be feeling about what was happening to me. I did not want to know anything. I did not care. After all, I was the one who was sick, I was in need of care, and if they wanted to have a problem with this, if for some reason it served them, let them handle it themselves.

The surgeon, a very kind man, seemed to understand my position and sympathise with me. He often talked to me and I understood that he was trying to get me to express myself, to take a part of my burden off me. "Don't be afraid, my girl!" he said. "Nothing will happen to you again, you'll see". His words, however, instead of relieving me, angered me even more because they gave me the impression that he considered me foolish and that he was mocking me while trying to make me believe them. Consequently, I did not even talk to him, I did not open my heart to tell him of my pain.

The surgery took place soon after and the histological examination that followed was positive. It was indeed cancer which thankfully had not yet spread to other areas or organs. Confined to my hospital bed I puzzled for hours trying to answer questions born of my situation. I wondered what disease is, what cancer is. Why had it chosen me? What attracts it to certain organisms? Is there hope for a cure? How? When?

Behind all these agonising questions, of course, was the great fear, the fear of death, the fear of the loss of form; the fear that lurks insidiously inside every human heart, inside every human brain. How could I possibly be an exception and not feel it at a time, in fact, when everything was still so new and so sudden? I did not, however, realise this fear at the time and I transposed it onto other matters such as the questions about the disease and its treatment. To these I once gave myself a general answer, that I could not receive an explanation about such an important issue since I had never tackled it and had never studied anything similar that would give me the perceptions to help me understand it. Until finally, one day, as I was submerged, meditating and seeking some kind of answer, a thought flashed in my mind, a thought that after my persistent mental quests seemed to fall like a ripe fruit. And I heard a voice deep inside me say: "Everything is the natural consequence of the act preceding it."

New concerns began to make their appearance. Natural consequence? But of what? What had I done in the past that could have this terrible disease as its natural consequence? And how could someone lead a life without creating these physical consequences that would in turn make him or her experience their negative impacts? I sensed, however, vaguely, that this little phrase which had come from the depths of my inner self entailed the wisdom of truth and so I let myself go, confident in it, calming myself and hoping that at some point its particular meaning would be revealed to me.

I was released from the hospital and began to slowly regain my normal pace. My feelings of anger had by now softened up, and, without being completely dissolved, had given their place to other, milder ones. The daily chores forced me not to think too much about my problem and to let it gradually lose its edge through patience and hope. My husband helped me greatly with these internal adjustment procedures as he managed to not only hide his anguish for the development of my health, but to act as if nothing had happened. Psychology, also, helped me. A friend of mine had for years been taking group lessons on various psychological concepts and she suggested that I should join too. I thankfully listened to her and the lessons gave me exactly what I needed at the time, making me feel strong and useful again. They taught me to know myself, to reveal unknown aspects of myself, to better understand my behaviour towards other people as well as the behaviour of other people towards me.

What strongly characterised me at the time and had begun to emerge from my adolescence even, was a doubt concerning religion and a lack of faith in God. I was brought up in a family with Christian principles, with reverence and devotion to the divine, not with fanaticism and bigotry. I had not, however, validated these principles in a way needed in order to believe in them and accept them so that their impact on me would be beneficial and help me in the proper manifestation of my soul and personality.

Growing up and gaining a conscious recognition of the world around me, I kept feeling more and more irritated by certain issues which undermined my faith. What I could not accept, in particular, were the concepts of reward and punishment regarding religion. I perceived them in the narrow sense of their meaning and rebelled at the idea that I too would possibly be punished for something that I had committed and for which I was certain in advance that I could not have had bad intentions. I did not accept the view that there is purpose in someone undergoing the consequences of their actions and, even more, I could not understand that punishment and reward are within the human being, that they function in one's consciousness and that this is God.

A natural consequence of my negative position was lack of trust and aggressiveness towards religious things. The image of me was completed by the conceit I felt and the arrogant certainty that in this way I am truly free, independent of any commitments and restrictions. However, as if to fill and replenish the void created in my consciousness from my lack of faith, I felt a strong attraction towards the entity of Jesus whose teachings of love and compassion spoke directly to my soul and enlivened an undefined force within me.

Sometimes, blinded by my unreasonable egoism, which was fed by my negative reactions, I wondered why I felt this way. How should I interpret this deep positive influence that Jesus' teachings had on me? I did not in any way want to sense that I was committing myself, that I was losing what I wrongly, of course, considered as my inner freedom. And I reached the pitiful point where, instead of considering what was happening to me as the highest blessing, I would try to infect it with silly doubts and pose questions to myself such as: "Am I not as free as I think I am?" or "Is my spiritual freedom threatened and should I do something to save it?"

Time went by and I experienced the various events of my life, always maintaining the same position of denial regarding religious matters and faith in God but without particularly dealing with it. I had become accustomed to not resorting to invocations and prayers when I was in a difficult situation. I was, in fact, naive enough to believe that I could manage on my own, with my own personal strengths, even throughout the course of my illness, in all its painful stages.

Approximately three years had passed since the day I had started going to the psychology groups when I discovered a place where relaxation techniques were taught along with certain basic aspects of meditation. I was very interested in this knowledge and so I immediately enrolled in order to attend classes. I had a natural ability in relaxing and so I rapidly progressed. During a relaxation exercise, as I was submerged deep in myself and was open to anything, I suddenly had an image appear on the screen of my mind. I had not thought of it consciously nor had I mentally projected it, as usually happened with the relaxation exercises we performed, having in mind a certain idea to process. This image pictured the Apostles with the fiery tongues over their heads which I knew symbolised the Holy Spirit that Jesus passed on to His disciples. Why though had this vision come to me in this way? What did it want to tell me? Did it perhaps want to reveal my unconscious desire to change my position of non-belief that I held for years and believe in God again?

Within seconds I had the answer I was looking for. Like lightning a revelation flashed inside my consciousness and a power that came from the depth of my being shook me wholly. My body shivered and my soul rejoiced. "There is a God!" said the revelation. "He exists within you and you should believe in Him!"

Without needing any mental explanations at that time, without needing logical analyses, I immediately accepted that that is indeed how things are. And I understood that, along the years that had passed, my ability to find my faith, to seek union with God, had been unconsciously maturing and gradually preparing to manifest. The relaxation's calmness had helped me to communicate with my spiritual self, from where sprung the knowledge that I had unconsciously longed for so many years.

When the relaxation exercise ended, it was as if I had become a different person. I had not yet recovered from the thrill I had experienced, but I felt filled with a sense of security, assurance and completeness, the like of which I had never felt before. I knew, of course, that it was a sort of ecstasy, the intensity of which would soon be lost. But at the same time I knew with an unshakable certainty that faith in God's existence was finally and permanently established in my mind and heart, bringing about a new and important beginning to the course of my life, and that this faith would never again abandon me; a faith that I might never have had, if not for my disease that motivated me to search for my hidden powers and needs.

I could say that this was the first conscious step on the course I was about to follow, the course of spirituality, which, as I have already mentioned, is the unconscious goal in the life of every human being. I could also say that this whole event was a healing in the field of my consciousness, in the field of my soul, that – who knows? – may someday, also, bring my physical healing which I so strongly desired without confessing it. Then again, maybe it would show me somehow that the healing of the body is not as important as the "healing" of the soul.

OMILOS EKSIPIRETITON (THE SERVERS' SOCIETY) AND ITS TEACHING

Psychology and its lessons gave me all that they could give me and the time came when I felt that this circle was fully complete and had come to an end. As I also described in the previous chapter, a new cycle had already begun in my life, the cycle of relaxation and meditation, in its preliminary stages. Thanks to these new cycles I had regained my faith in God and I had begun praying again.

I had started to realise that the reason for which I was attracted this much to relaxation and meditation was the fact that I understood that they were another source of therapeutic help, apart from classical medicine, which had assisted me in the difficult days of my surgery and in which I would resort to again, if needed. I sensed that this source existed as an ability of my own self, as a power that would come out of me and lead me to control and direct, up to an extent, the state of my health.

Although I had no specific knowledge of this ability, something told me that it existed and that I would be given a way to get to know it and express it. The new field of faith that had opened up to me had sensitised my consciousness and I now felt an undefined power leading me to where I should go, so that I could reach the result that I now consciously sought.

That was how I found myself, in the early autumn of 1982, searching for Omilos Eksipiretiton (the Servers' Society) in the area of Patisia. I had been informed by a friend of mine that this Society was a spiritual centre, a school of practical philosophy whose founder, whom everybody called Master, taught the spiritual principles of love, mutual respect, selfless offer, faith to God, and more. My friend also told me that the older members of the Society, who were close to the Master, tried to implement these principles as much as possible.

I was impressed! Could it be true? Was there actually a place so close to me, so easily accessible, where one could find such an atmosphere? It was impossible for me to not doubt it and to not have questions. I decided, however, to let things go their own way hoping that the truth would be revealed to me at some point, through the experiences and the contact I would have with the people of the Society and, particularly, with the Master.

On the day that I decided to go to the Society, I had some concerns thinking that it might not be so simple or easy for someone to visit him, that maybe certain conditions were required in order to get to know its members and meet its founder. With great pleasure I realised from the very first moment that there was no reason for these fears and misgivings. The door was open to anyone who wanted to come in, the people were willing to accept you and talk to you, to answer any questions you had, to provide you with any information you asked for. As for the Master, he was, also, very willing to unfold all the aspects of his teaching, to explain and convey it without getting tired or resentful, as one of his key objectives was to open to those seeking, even unconsciously, the road to spirituality, the road to God. It was a blessing that, due to the small number of the Society's members at the time, as it was at the start of its founding, the Master had enough time for us. So, we all had the opportunity to be close to him often and to listen to his beneficial words, which fell as balm into the thirsty for truth consciences of those who approached him for help.

With my daily presence at the Society but, mainly, with the frequent hearing of the Master's words, the questions and doubts I had gradually declined, losing their strength. The assurance and validation that I needed to fully persuade me of the teaching was given from the Master's actions, from the interest he showed in everyone, his responsiveness and his love. The Master genuinely expressed the eternal spiritual principles that he taught and represented, tirelessly conveying them as a conduit between God and humans, making these principles more accessible to their level and making himself a living example of their application.

Two years had passed since the founding of the Society in the summer of 1980 when I found myself within it. During this time, the Master had been preparing his older disciples who would be responsible for helping him in the task of spreading the teachings. Their preparation was intense. How could they teach those who came and help in solving their problems, if they had not first worked on their own equilibrium, if their soul's tranquillity had not emerged from within them, so that they could in turn pass it on to those who sought it?

Alongside the training of the older disciples, new study groups were soon created for the newer members of the Society. These were called "Self Study" groups because that was the purpose of their existence, self-knowledge. They primarily sought to build proper relationships between the individuals and, also, between every individual and oneself. These groups were undertaken by the older disciples, always under the guidance of the Master. From the very first day they started, I too joined a group and began attending the courses. I had previously gone through a similar discipleship with psychology and relaxation but here there was something much deeper and much more meaningful. There was the concept of the Spirit, which we are called to reveal from the depths of our existence, and there was our connection with God, which we had to acknowledge within ourselves. In short, there was more of a practical than theoretical spirituality with all of its associated issues, for which, it is true, I always had a very vague idea – and I wasn't the only one – considering them incomprehensible and inaccessible. The way, however, in which these subjects were approached at the Society's courses, was unlike any other discipleship of mine. These courses sought to familiarise individuals with these higher ideas and to help them unite directly with them through the cultivation and broadening of their minds, but, also, at the same time, through the opening of their hearts.

The Master provided his teaching in a simple way, merging all the spiritual principles that had been given to humanity and that had moulded its morals and cultures. As we moved through our discipleship, I validated all the more the truth of this teaching which of course I could only understand and apply to a certain extent, as these concepts are great and absolute. I could see with pleasure, however, that the teaching I was receiving was slowly sensitising me so that my ability to understand it progressively grew, making me an even more positive recipient of it.

The Master said that the human being must have noble ideals and goals not only for oneself, but for all of humanity; to believe in spiritual evolution and to work for the good of the whole. He used Socrates' high dialectical method to prove and simplify the teachings at the same time. Only when those concepts were passed into our conscience, would we be able to apply them in our life as he did. It was not enough to grasp them and understand, for example, what "I voice my opinion freely" or "I respect the opinion of others" means; we had to be able to constantly apply these concepts. Only then would the Society fulfil its goal as a practical philosophy school where individuals, understanding the eternal concepts of wisdom and truth, would see their practical demonstration in everyday life.

One of the main goals of the teaching at the Society is for individuals to know themselves. In other words, to be aware of what is happening to them at every moment, what they are thinking, what they are feeling, what they want as well being aware of the true causes governing their actions; to also know how to consciously handle the energies and forces of the soul. For this goal to be achieved by the disciples, it is not enough for them to briefly read or to hear the texts of the courses written in the special booklets. It needs constant, systematic work with perseverance and patience, which gradually brings the desired result while compensating for the effort.

The means for this work are meditation and observation. Of meditation, I already had a certain knowledge and more or less knew what it was, as I also did with relaxation. What disconcerted me, causing me many difficulties, until finally understanding it, was the function of self-observation, the so-called observer. This observer must be neutral and detached from any criticism, self-control and subjective impressions. One simply observes oneself – since the observer and the subject of observation are the same person – and then records the observations without judging or criticizing.

I found it really hard to learn how to function in such a neutral way. To observe, without being influenced from what I saw myself doing, thinking, and feeling. The rest of the trainees also had the same difficulty with me, but, when they understood the function of self-observation, they recognised how much it helped and redeemed them.

"Self-observation reveals hidden fears, negative thoughts," a member wrote down in his folder, "and that helps me a lot with the function of self-knowledge."

Another member had written: "My observer has become automatic. It works constantly, with no resistances, no effort. It has helped me greatly."

Another member confessed the difficulty he had before starting his discipleship at the Society: "I still cannot forget the self-check I used to perform every night before sleeping which made me lose my sleep many times. Now, with the observer, things have changed. I discern and appreciate the positive aspects of myself."

With the help of the observer, an individual can change oneself, if one decides to. But how is this change made? The answer to this question is: "We do not resist what we find; we leave things to their own flow. Gradually, the effects of change come by themselves. We simply observe without interfering."

I elaborated more on the observer as an element of teaching because it is the start-up of self-knowledge. Equally important are all the other elements such as relaxation, meditation, awareness of the energy's flow within the body, expression and control of emotions, the manifestation of love, the development of the mind. To these I will refer to in more detail as I move on to the narrative of the various experiences and events that I will describe in the book. And, of course, to all of these we must also add spiritual healing.

Today, after many years of discipleship, I have reached the conclusion that the "Servers' Society" could, also, be called the "Society of Spiritual Healing", in the broadest sense, meaning the adjustment of a disturbed equilibrium in any field through spirituality. It also means the recognition of the divine power, which all beings carry within us, and its conscious use by human beings for the solution of the various problems in everyday life: health, work, relationships, etc. This is the goal of the teaching given to me by the Master and which all of his disciples pass on to all other members of the Society.

INTRODUCTION TO
SPIRITUAL HEALING

The Society's Master, in his effort to help his fellow human, was not content on only organising groups through which the teaching could be provided and spirituality would spread. "The needs are many," he used to say, "and people need help immediately in order to cope with their difficulties."

For this reason he created early on a separate section within the Society, the section of spiritual healing. This consisted of a small group with three of his oldest disciples, those who had shown a special appeal for this vocation and had proven their healing abilities with their actions.

The person in charge of the healing section at the time was the Master himself. When a difficult patient's case presented itself, he always helped the group of spiritual healers towards the soundest completion of the healing process, either by giving his advice on what had to be done, or by undertaking the healing process himself. He had healed many patients and these successes had astonished me when I was informed of them in the beginning. It was one of the reasons that made me rush to him in the hope that he could, also, heal me and that one day he could perhaps accept me as a spiritual healer and teach me how to heal myself and others.

At the beginning of the founding of the Society's healing section, the Master focused more on the training of the spiritual healers. His aim was to build and consolidate within them the principles of the teaching by raising their spiritual level, improving their performance and strengthening their internal powers. He wanted to render them, as soon as possible, autonomous and active in the performance of their work since they had shown that they were in a position to achieve positive healing results and had offered themselves up to the service of spiritual healing. Their own progress would also help the patients who trusted the course of their therapy to the healing section.

I was one of those patients, too. After the surgery I had undergone ten years ago, my body seemed to be considerably weakened and, although it had been so long since then, it still exhibited certain small but bothersome symptoms. My neck hurt and my legs had internal and external varicose veins which also hurt and presaged the manifestation of phlebitis. I had already enlisted the help of Homoeopathy which had helped me remarkably for two years. The symptoms, however, had reappeared as I had neglected to take my medications for a while. I decided, therefore, to address the spiritual healing section of the Society. I was curious to see the outcome of the healers' effort. Would they cure the symptoms temporarily? Would they be able to permanently eliminate them or would they, in the worst case, not affect them at all?

On the appointed time and day I arrived at the Society feeling various emotions, but, especially, eagerness as I was in a hurry to finally get to see up close a more comprehensive form of spiritual healing. I had already formed a vague idea of it from the rudimentary lessons I had taken in the form of relaxation. The healers led me to a room and there, as I had been warned, was another patient waiting, a young man with advanced cancer. His face, his attitude, the way he sat, revealed desperation and fear. We sat next to each other and I felt that I wanted very much to do something to relieve him.

There was a tranquillity and calmness in the room that deeply permeated me, giving me confidence in the spiritual healing and the spiritual healers who took their places opposite us and prepared to begin their work. I wondered what they would do. Would they place their hands on us? Would we be made to do something? And would we do it correctly?

The person in charge of our group guided us to relaxation and soon the healers were at work. Their procedure was actually quite simple and silent, far from impressive or unfamiliar. I quickly relaxed in body and mind and at some point a prayer spontaneously appeared in my mind. I started repeating it, again and again, and that helped me focus on the proceedings, a fact that, as I understood, helped facilitate the work of the healers who continued to work in absolute silence opposite us.

As I was immersed, I had a feeling of something resembling electrical current, an energy, passing from the healers to me, permeating me wholly, rejuvenating me and invigorating my tired cells. I enjoyed this feeling and I wanted to believe that the pleasure it caused would also heal me. Suddenly, I had the notion of myself participating in my own treatment and attempting to apply what little I had learned. "Would I be able to do it?" I wondered.

I mentally brought the image of myself in front of me, as I had been taught at the Society's relaxation courses, and visualised myself within a bright sun whose brightness passed through all of my points. As a novice in this procedure, I could not perform it properly and every now and then my thoughts got off track. In addition, there was a tension and a desire within me to succeed that kept me from functioning freely. As I later learned, these emotions should not exist in spiritual healers, as they make them persistently pursue a positive result, without letting themselves to the will of God, for only He can decide on the healing or not of a patient.

I do not know how much time had passed when I felt the need to interrupt the healing I was performing on myself and look at the sick man beside me. His eyes were closed and his face seemed calm, even though he looked in as much pain as before. I thought then that I could perform a healing on him, too, as I had performed on myself. I brought him in front of me with my thought, also visualising him within a bright sun and tried to remain focused on this image as much as I could.

Shortly thereafter, the healers told us to open our eyes and to stop the relaxation, as they had completed their work. They gave thanks to the Almighty and asked us if we wanted to say something, if we had perceived something special during the healing or if we felt any difference in our bodies. I told them that I was not able at that time to discern if or how much the bothersome symptoms had decreased. I did, however, feel lightened and refreshed, as if a weight and a charge had been lifted from me and I was finally relieved of their presence. The other patient mentioned that he had calmed down quite a bit and that the pain had somewhat softened.

When he left, I described to the healer in charge of the group what I had done as faithfully as I could. I was anxious to hear what she would tell me. Had I acted correctly? As soon as I finished the narration, she smiled and told me that this initiative was a very positive sign that I was truly interested in spiritual healing and that perhaps soon I too would be joining the healing group.

My own healing continued for a while by the group of spiritual healers, simply and calmly each time, but without the feeling of excitement that I had felt on the first day. My healers explained to me that this was not important and that the healing was performed anyway. The symptoms were indeed reduced to a minimum so the healing was deemed to be finished. In a few days they had completely disappeared and did not return ever again.

This fact played a crucial role in my spiritual advancement and gave me the message that spiritual healing would take a special place in my life, as I had discovered on my own body its ability to favourably influence simple pathological symptoms and – why not? – possibly even serious conditions. This I would later find out as spiritual healer I had decided to request to become.

THE TRAINING
OF SPIRITUAL HEALERS

Within a relatively short period of time from the day I started following the "Self Study" courses and having lived through the valuable experience of my healing which had a catalytic effect on me, I, too, asked to be included in the healing group and considered it an honour to be accepted. My training as a spiritual healer started that moment. That meant that, along with the courses intended for all members and which were also necessary for the healers so that the principles of the teaching were consolidated within them, I also followed special courses given by the Master.

The number of healers had now increased and so had the number of patients who came for help as the healing group's positive reputation kept growing and spreading. The newest of us, who were also the majority, were at an experimental stage. We each had our own experiences, due to the differences between us concerning the period of our discipleship. Although we were considered – and we were – "under testing", we participated in the functions of the group with the older healers. They had undertaken our guidance and tried to pass on to us their experience, alongside the courses given to us by the Master.

An issue which we examined greatly as trainees in spiritual healing, but also as ordinary disciples of the Society's teachings, was the recognition of our spiritual nature. After a period of study and practice on it, we managed to grasp it mentally, some more than others, depending on each person's abilities. We still, however, had to conquer its hardest part, not only to believe and accept that we have the power of the Spirit within us, the power of God that exists equally within all beings of the universe, but to also consciously experience this power. To feel it flow through our body, transformed into its individual energies and powers that spring only through it and maintain the perpetual becoming. To observe it taking on different forms within us and within others and becoming at times thoughts and feelings, at times love and healing, and at times work, joy, and even grief, in our everyday life. And, finally, to learn to handle it with our own will, guiding it to where it is needed each time, particularly as a healing power towards people who are suffering.

This is an issue that, as all the so-called internal issues, those pertaining to the "ubiquitous" presence of God in the universe, cannot be exhausted by a single understanding, recognition or realisation. Our training on it had only just begun. The small realisations we had made, through the appropriate sensitisation of the mind and heart, gave us just the spark for the decision to work steadily, but it was accompanied with a continuous questioning. Like all who deal with spirituality, spiritual healers constantly practice on union with God. And this has no end.

Spiritual healing, healing through the Spirit. Spiritual healing is the predominant application of conscious and deliberate use of the power of the Spirit to provide aid and service to humanity by spiritual healers around the world. The spiritual healers can see within themselves the Entity, God, and they can see it within the patients being healed, too. The difference between the two is that, while the healers manage to be more and more consciously united with God, the patients, on the other hand, are unconsciously united. They do not realise the power of

God within them and do not know how to use it in helping themselves. This task is the responsibility of the healers, consciously channelling the healing power to the patients, an assistance that they cannot give to themselves.

"Spiritual healing is actually a healing that is performed by the Entity to the Entity" the Master said. The Entity, God, is diffused everywhere, it is within the healer, it is also within the patient, it is the healer and the patient, it is the divine Power that performs the healing. Advancing in one's evolutionary course, the healer is increasingly consolidated on this fundamental principle, that healing is not performed by oneself but by God and His will. The healer is nothing but His conscious conduit. And this the healer experiences as a feeling of mergence with the unified divine field, a sublime and unique feeling which floods him or her wholly and which is also felt vibrating the body and soul of the patient, to whom the healer radiates the healing energy.

I would like to make a small parenthesis here and refer to something purely practical that will assist the readers in the understanding of this book. As they read it, they will frequently encounter various words whose significance they might not fully understand. These words are nothing more than different names of God, such as Entity, Ontological Self, Creator, Creative Principle, Higher Power, Essence, Absolute, Source of Life, Superego and possibly others, too.

One of the most important tasks among those assigned by the Master to the "under testing" healers to whom I too belonged, was the following: in order to prove that we can indeed be spiritual healers, capable and worthy to undertake this important vocation, we must find ten patients each. We must then regularly perform healing on them in the same way we did for the patients treated by the Society's healing group. Finally, we must make a small personal file in which we would record various details on the progress of the patients, such as the diversification – if any – of the expert opinions of their doctors, their improvement or deterioration as well as any other information that might come up.

Despite the kindness and love the Master showed us whenever he entrusted us with something, I felt a kind of panic. Was my soul's inclination as much as I declared it to be? Was my offer of devotion and service to my fellow people truly selfless? Would the Master finally accept me as a spiritual healer or would he reject me as inadequate? And was I truly a spiritual healer? The Society's teaching, of course, declares that all people can become spiritual healers, that everyone is a spiritual healer, they are just not aware of it because of their ignorance of the spiritual power inherent in the depth of their being.

That is what theory says. But what happens in practice? We all mentally accepted and understood this theory. It was, however, too soon to experience it in our conscience, to believe in it without vacillations and to consciously recognise the spiritual background of our human existence. With the task that the Master assigned to us, he wanted to increasingly mobilise us in realising our spiritual nature and to prove to ourselves that we can succeed as healers. He knew for certain, without telling us, that we, first and foremost, needed this proof to strengthen our confidence and to be able to work with greater faith during the healing.

On the same day that I was accepted as an "under testing" healer, something strange happened. Various patients started approaching me in my personal life, talking to me about their illnesses and, directly or indirectly, asking for my help. At the time I couldn't explain the synchronism of their call for help with my need to find patients to heal. Later, however, and with the teaching I received, I understood the cause of this event. It is the unity and inner communication between individuals, on the mental and spiritual level, which causes this coordination, as I will refer to in following chapters in detail. Although I could not explain what was happening, I considered this massive turnout of patients unconsciously attracted to my decision to work on the expression of spiritual healing a blessing at the time. And I felt joy in suggesting to them a healing method different from those they had tried up to then.

It was not easy convincing patients to accept the idea of spiritual healing, something which most had never heard of before. But I had so much thirst in my soul and I had taken my duty towards the Master and towards spiritual healing itself – which I wanted to serve no matter what – so seriously, that their reactions did not stop me. I started to knowingly become even intrusive at times in order to achieve their consent and start working with them. Indeed, in the end I succeeded. The ill ended up accepting my offer.

In my discipleship folder from those days, there is a short prayer that reveals my inner state.

"Lord, I wish to humbly serve You through spiritual healing. I humbly wish to serve my fellow people through it. If my desire agrees with Your own will, set forth, please, from within me my healing potential and make me worthy to relieve their various needs, to ease their pain. Thank Thee, Lord!"

The rest of the healer trainee group had similar dealings with the issue. They had a strong desire of the soul to serve spiritual healing and a concern, as they often said, that they might not succeed. We all worked feverishly as the healings of the patients that each of us had undertaken to heal on our own were now added to the healings we were already performing on the Society's patients. The methods we used for the healing of these patients were the same as those we applied at the Society.

Other times we worked "from a distance" when patients were not present and other times we worked "on contact" when they could be with us. I will refer to these methods gradually over the following chapters.

One of the problems I faced at that time was the indifference of patients to inform me of their health. I had struggled greatly to achieve a proper communication with them. This happened because they were probably not accustomed to the concept of spiritual healing, even though they had eventually accepted it, and they had not yet realised the importance it could have on restoring their health. It seems, however, that I too did not assume the right stance towards them. The will of my soul was too close to the desire of my ego to succeed and prove that I healed the sick whom I had undertaken each time. That is why I seemed impatient and in a hurry to receive regular and frequent updates which, of course, I hoped were positive, not only for the benefit of the patients but also for my satisfaction, considering the cure a personal success.

This attitude definitely unconsciously charged the patients and disoriented them. It made them resist to a wrong function – my own function – rendering the communication between us unable to find its correct expression. The solution to this problem, which was common to all novice healers, as we ourselves confessed, was our change of attitude. It was the realisation of our error and the gradual elimination of our need to repeat it, to want to appropriate the success of the healing so as to satisfy our personal ego.

All of us "under testing" healers wanted to reach the point of properly dealing with a healing, something that we theoretically knew how to do. In practice, however, we had not yet expressed this attitude. This happened gradually, over the years, with the experiences we gained and the teaching we continuously received. A teaching that was not limited only to the knowledge and methods of healing but that gradually lead us to our induction in spirituality, to the union with the Entity, and to the firm position of the healer.

Spiritual healing needs simplicity, serenity, faith and no doubts, no haste or impatience for results, it needs the awareness, as I mention above, that healing is provided not by the spiritual healer but from the divine source, the Almighty. The great English healer Harry Edwards said on spiritual healing that "it needs abandonment, not effort." With these words he meant that the spiritual healer, when working for the patient, should not push and try, but let himself or herself to the divine Will, which decides on the final and definitive outcome of the healing.

THE FIRST HEALINGS

The success of our healing work had an incredible progress during our training. For the learning period that we were undergoing, it was very heartening to see our efforts bring positive results. They were simple and easy cases of course, but for us it had great value to see a headache, for example, disappear within a few minutes and a toothache or a sore throat to go away or even anger to subside or, in fact, anything else that came along, to almost always be settled. If, after this settlement we still considered the issue wanting, we would also refer the "patients" to medical science, if they had not already resorted to it on their own, so as to determine the cause of the problem and deal with it accordingly. For example, a toothache that had passed should have its cause investigated, as the problematic tooth might need to be filled or removed and so on.

A complete healing during that learning period was the healing of a very strong headache, which had been bothering an acquaintance of mine for three whole days, and who was healed immediately. I regularly passed by his workshop at the time, as I was working with him on a particular issue.

"I have had a terrible headache for three days now that will not let me work," he complained one afternoon when I was at his workshop. I immediately wondered if I should offer to perform spiritual healing on him. As a novice I was hesitant to try. Would he be willing to accept it? And if he accepted it, would he let me perform what I knew or would he doubt something he did not know, resisting, clenching up and not letting the headache pass?

Within a few seconds, a series of conflicting thoughts came back and forth in my mind until I made the decision for the final step. And I eventually made it. Whatever his reaction would be, I thought, positive or negative, as a spiritual healer that I was, even a novice, I knew what I had to do to relieve him and I had to try, no matter what the final result would be. The Master had told us that the spiritual healer is God's servant, ready at any moment to provide for any need that appears on his or her path, whether it concerned health or other issues, and ready to accept the settlement that the Almighty designated.

Something, however, was still holding me back. My personal desire to succeed and the fear of my potential failure. Functions both selfish and adverse to the basic principle that the healer is taught, the detachment from the result of one's work. At that time, however, I did not have the necessary experience, I was not quite entrenched in the vocation and was swayed by somewhat unclear incentives. I immediately realised my mistake and remembered the healer's duty to offer help beyond limits and conditions. So without any doubt or hesitation I opened my mouth and asked him:

"Would you want me to perform spiritual healing on you? It is very likely that the headache will pass."

He accepted immediately, only asking me a few questions first, which was, of course, entirely natural. He wanted to know what spiritual healing was, what he would have to do, what I would do, etc. I assured him that he did not have to do anything at all and that the only thing I asked of him was to quietly sit in his office chair.

The door to the workshop was open, the street crowded and noisy, with cars constantly coming and going, and the chance of someone coming in or passing by and seeing us was high. From the moment, however, that I decided with a clear mind-set to help him, I was sure that no external element would intervene or interrupt us. The Entity, which I was serving from that moment on, would take care of it. I could ask him to close the door or even to lock it, so that no-one would disturb us, but I did not want to let him think that something strange was about to happen. I wanted him to view it as something simple and let himself open up, accepting the healing.

I prepared for the "contact" healing by performing all that I had been taught at the Society. I stood upright behind him and told him to close his eyes and relax as much as possible. In the courses on spiritual healing we were taught that in cases such as this one, where the patients are ignorant of such matters they cannot usually relax on their own. It is therefore necessary for us to guide them on how to perform a small relaxation before the healing. Here, however, I did not want the process to take too long, as Peter* would definitely become aggravated because I was distracting him from his work, even if it was for his own good. Apart from that, although I was a novice, I still had a hunch that he would manage to relax on his own quite easily, which he did.

I closed my eyes to concentrate better and placed my joined palms above his head, without touching it. Inter-

---

* The name «Peter» as well as all the names that will be used for patients are not their actual names. I simply borrow them for each person, so that there is the necessary discretion in each case.

nally I had assumed the correct state, imagining that I function as God's conduit and not of my own accord. I invoked the divine Power to help accomplish the healing, in order to relieve this man, but also to help him understand, if possible, the concept of spiritual healing so that his soul can be awakened, fundamentally helping him.

I felt deeply united with God, I felt my soul communicate with Peter's soul and I constantly brought to my mind the vision that the healing power permeated my body and was channelled to his own, balancing the anomaly that existed within his head. I visualised these divine powers becoming light and that this light, after passing entirely through him, reached into his head, where it caused a mobilisation of the energies gathered there, possibly because of his multitude of thoughts or because of some other problem which had caused the intensity and pain. Then I visualised myself directing these energies with the help of the light, moving them from the points where they were trapped and guiding them out, passing through my hands. I constantly referred to the Entity, to God, and let myself to His guidance.

At one point I realised that I was functioning mildly and that the attraction of the energies from Peter's head was not being completed. I realised that my communication with the Entity and my focus in the healing work had slackened. I instantly recovered and concentrated my attention with greater awareness on performing my internal work. At once, I felt myself essentially participating again as my hands absorbed the excess energy that was released from its sanctuary, Peter's aching head, and dissipated in the form of intense heat. Beams of heat left the "patient's" head towards the healer's hands that were accordingly warmed, as they absorbed it before releasing it. These beams were taking a specific form within my internal field of vision. Behind my closed eyelids, I clearly "saw" waves of energy going upwards, just as I had visualised it. This internal "vision" potentially exists within every human being and can be perceived by the spiritual healers helping them accomplish their work, as we had been taught in the courses taken as trainee healers.

I continued the healing until I felt the energy diminishing and my hands slowly cooling. I asked Peter how he felt and he said that his headache was completely gone. My hands, as if to confirm this, were no longer drawing any more energy, evidence that they had absorbed the excess quantity, which had dissipated outwards, leaving Peter's head free from the burden that had been pressing it. The healing had come to an end.

I thanked the Lord for His help and told Peter that the healing was complete, a fact that he had realised himself, as his headache had disappeared. His surprise was so great, that for a moment he lost his voice, looking at me as if petrified. He could not understand how it was possible for such an intense and debilitating headache that had lasted three whole days and who knows how many more, to go away just like that, within only ten minutes.

"But what did you do to me?" he asked again and again. "What is this spiritual healing? I will come to the Society one day and see up close how you train to achieve these wonderful results." I told him we that we would happily accept him and that I was available if he needed my help again.

The complete healing I described above was not the only one performed by the healers during our trial period. Everyone had similar examples to show. I will mention one of them, which I think is very characteristic.

Ellie, a spiritual healer, has a son who was four and a half years old, when his mother was a member of the "under testing" healers. One day, he started having intense pains in his groin area and the doctor examining him found a hernia, specifically an inguinal hernia. The bulge could be felt by palpation, and was even visible, too, so the doctor deemed it necessary that the child be examined by a surgeon. Indeed, a surgeon examined Nikos, making the same exact diagnosis.

Ellie began monitoring her son and realised that the lump appeared after intense activity and playing. Before going back to the surgeon to decide when to operate on Nikos, Ellie considered performing spiritual healing on the child. She placed her hand on Nikos' body, on the spot where the hernia was, and visualised all the intensity there, pressing her hand, focusing on it, and, with the help of the Divine Grace, it began dissolving and spreading out. She focused on the healing for a long time, as she could internally see that it was what she had to do, until, at one point, she felt the swelling under her hand calming and deflating. She then realised that the surgery was no longer necessary.

The next morning, they went to the appointment with the surgeon where the child, after being thoroughly examined, was found to no longer have any discernible bulge. To be sure, the doctor recommended special child stress-tests, in order to see if the hernia would reappear again after fatigue or intense play. For one week Nikos' mother along with his doctors monitored him on a daily basis, but no discomfort or bulge reappeared. Since then Nikos played and got tired just like any other child, without any symptom of his hernia appearing again.

"After this experience," said the satisfied mother, "I validated the positive effect of spiritual healing and its potential for permanent effectiveness." At the same time, the Master validated her ability to become a spiritual healer along with the rest of the healers.

Before concluding this chapter, I would like to present a healing performed by another, also under testing, healer. A friend of this healer, Aristides, had been leisurely driving his car, when suddenly he felt a strong jolt and realised that his body had undergone a shock. In a split second he realised what had happened. A car had run into his and had shaken him. The areas hurt mostly were his neck and the upper part of his spine. Those who have suffered a similar jolt know how terrible it is and how much fear it causes for any consequences that might possibly follow. Aristides was just as scared. And what he first thought of doing was to enlist the aid of his friend, who was one of the Society's spiritual healers, who later recounted to me all parts of the healing performed, just as I convey it here.

Aristides sat quietly in a chair while the healer made the usual preparations in order to join the Entity. Soon he (the healer) had the feeling of "seeing" what was going on inside his friend's neck. And what he saw looked like a proper battlefield, where forces, reminiscent of elemental beings, crowded one on top of the other, as if to show their presence, trying to earn their place in the patient's body. The healer mentally brought a bright light onto this field, the light of the sun, but without radiating, without in other words focusing any particular power, so as not to increase the intensity already present, he started channelling a current of tranquillity.

The healer realised that the intensity was greater in the upper left part of his friend's neck, where the skull bones begin. He questioned Aristides about this who indeed confirmed it. He continued enlightening the sore points and "saw" the disrupted powers gradually arranging, bringing themselves to order and calming. Within ten minutes at the most, the agitation of the cells had been settled and an order, which we could call ritualistic, had been restored. Everything had taken its place in that particular part of the body, the place given by the Maker when creating them.

The healer stayed for a little while longer behind Aristides, feeling for himself the tranquillity that had passed into the agitated areas and only when he considered this tranquillity stabilised, did he conclude the healing. The patient, however, was not yet fully relieved, something that sometimes happens in spiritual healing. It takes a period of one or more hours for the result to show. Indeed, so it happened with Aristides. By evening there was no longer any discomfort in his neck from this unpleasant experience. Of course, this healer was also officially accepted by the Master and was considered a proven spiritual healer.

The healers' ability to realise the state of their patients is of course surprising to the reader, as indeed it is surprising to the healers themselves, especially in the early stages of their work. Interpreting this fact, the Master says the following:

"Humans, as social beings, are in contact with a group of people and act and participate in it either within their family or within any other, limited or not, social event. Consequently, they exchange with others energies and powers of their spirit and soul through their natural body. They give and receive the good and the bad, disease and health, but they are not aware of exactly what is happening to them at any given moment. People, as is known, resemble communicating vessels. The energies and powers from one are transferred to the other, returning back where they came from and so on. This, however, happens for the most part unconsciously.

The spiritual healers who work continuously for their communication and union with God, become increasingly conscious of the energies and powers of the soul, recognising in them the living processes of the Spirit. By the Divine Grace they are given the opportunity to receive the answers they need to perform the healing. Beyond seeing the body internally in its every detail, they can also make an accurate diagnosis for every condition and its cause, as well as the methods of healing that should be applied, both in clinical medicine and spiritual healing. This ability increases depending on the degree of union between the spiritual healers and the Higher Self, God, who is equally inside them and the patients."

HEALING ON THE EFFECTS OF CHEMOTHERAPY

As I mentioned in the previous chapter, our successes with the patients whom we had individually undertaken as novice spiritual healers were considered very satisfactory by the Master in this stage of our advancement. Thus, his official and definitive approval to join the Society's group of spiritual healing was given to us all. Our expectations and hopes had finally been achieved and we could stop agonising over our concern that we might not be accepted. Our dedication to the vocation and the inclination that we had showed towards it from the beginning, became all the more our conscious trait, helping us in our work. Of course, there were many elements still left for us to realise and accomplish.

From now on, however, we could be entrusted with more serious and difficult cases as we constantly gained in our abilities to succeed with the passage of time. So, along with the small and simple daily healings we continuously performed, once in a while we also carried out more complicated ones, using as much as we could of the knowledge the Master had provided us with. We worked either in groups, with the healings we undertook at the Society's relevant section, or individually, with the healings that patients requested of us, often unexpectedly. This could happen with a phone call that we received at home, with a random incident in the street, in a vehicle or, in fact, anywhere else. As we have often mentioned, the spiritual healer is ready at any moment to serve whatever need might occur.

In the lines that follow, I describe the healing of a patient who appeared unexpectedly, desperately seeking the help of spiritual healing. She would indeed receive it in an impressive way.

It was a day like any other. I was coming and going inside the house, doing my housework, when at one point the phone rang. I heard a distressed and confused voice that I did not immediately recognise.

"Mrs Kiki, please help me! I am in despair, I do not know what to do. I cannot breathe, my body will not obey me and I am shivering throughout. My hands and my feet have turned outwards!"

I was shocked! Something like this had never happened to me before; so immediate, so urgent and serious. I had never encountered such panic as a spiritual healer. I soon realised that the girl calling me in so much agony was Maria who just a few days ago had undergone a cancer hysterectomy and was now receiving chemotherapy. Maria attended courses at a self-study group and showed a strong inclination for the teaching and its spiritual principles. When the doctors announced to her their initial diagnosis, she anxiously came to the Society seeking the help of spiritual healing. She recognised that the healing she was receiving helped her greatly in accepting the extent of her ordeal with serenity and bravery, despite her young age and her only recent marriage.

As soon as I received her call that day, I immediately realised that Maria's present condition was clearly due to the well-known painful side effects of chemotherapy. Without asking her for explanations, as I did not want to waste time, I hastily tried to reassure her, telling her that I would do whatever I could. We hanged up the phone and I retired to the room I used for performing all my internal tasks, meditations, healings etc.

I delved into myself and concentrated on the patient. I mentally brought her in front of me and "enveloped" her with my thoughts in a clear, glowing light, imagining this light to be the power of God, the power of love and healing that permeated all parts of her body, in order to cleanse them. On my mind's screen, Maria became light-filled, proof that she was receptive to the radiance, to the light I was sending her, as had been proven from the healing that she was already receiving from the group.

I then visualised the power of God, like a tranquil current, passing into her and completely overwhelming her. It passed through all her organs, all her cells and dragged with it, depositing on the ground all useless elements and toxins created not only from the influence of the powerful drugs but also from the negative feelings of fear and panic that had overcome her. I repeated this healing regimen several times. At the same time, I invoked the divine power to influence the function of the healing in helping the chemotherapy do its work on Maria's health as best it could.

My work lasted about a quarter of an hour. When focused on their work, spiritual healers gradually develop an intuition that shows them when the healing is complete for that particular occasion. After that there is nothing more for them to do, regardless of any apparent effects on the patients. So, as soon as I too felt that the healing was complete, without of course knowing what had happened to the patient, I proceeded to thank the Lord and resume my housework. My mind, however, was constantly on the patient trying to visualise her inside the light.

I expected that Maria would soon ring to joyfully announce her healing to me and provide me with all the extra information which I had willingly avoided asking for previously. The phone, however, did not ring, and I kept wondering why. What could possibly be happening to her? Has she been healed, but considered it unnecessary to announce it to me, thinking perhaps that I was not particularly interested, or was she still in her previous state and was so disappointed that she did not want to contact me? Intuitively, however, I felt that she was well and had recovered but I needed her confirmation to validate this intuition.

Finally, the phone rang. It was indeed Maria, thrilled, touched and grateful for the results of the spiritual healing. Calm at last, she described to me in detail the course of her healing that only lasted a few minutes. As soon as she put the phone down, following our initial call, and after the short time which she estimated it took for me to begin the healing, the first painful symptoms began receding. Her hands and feet regained their normal position, her breathing found its calm rhythm and a sweet tranquillity spread throughout her body, soon passing deeper into her emotional world and soul. The panic disappeared completely and Maria finally regained herself.

I asked her to talk to me about the reason for this crisis; what did she think had caused it, and she then told me the whole story. The previous day she had undergone chemotherapy at the hospital and everything had gone well. Her doctor, however, gave her a prescription for a drug that she should take, an antidote against any side effects that might occur. He stressed that this drug was the only one suitable for her case and that she should take it without question, as without it she would very likely experience major discomforts. Maria did not listen to him, believing that she would be able to handle on her own anything that came her way. But things were not as she anticipated. Chemotherapy is not a joke.

Scared and panicked, she saw her body being affected more and more by the treatment she had undergone and felt powerless to do anything about it. She then sent a cousin of hers, who happened to be at their home, to buy the drug. But where to find it? It was Saturday and the pharmacies were closed. Having searched in vain for one on duty, he finally started for the hospital where Maria's doctor worked, hoping to find him and the life-saving medicine there. During his absence, Maria called me and asked for the help of spiritual healing – a little late to say the truth. This delay, as she explained, was because she was not able at that time, due to her terribly difficult situation, to talk to her cousin about spiritual healing and analyse what it is and how it works, something that he would surely ask. So, instead, she patiently waited for something to happen that would give her the opportunity to quietly make the desired phone call which she firmly believed would cure her. And, finally, she had the chance, as soon as he left.

The doctor at the hospital had the drug that Maria needed and gave it to her cousin. By the time it got to her, however, she no longer needed it. And she did not take it neither at that time nor later since the symptoms of the side effects had completely disappeared.

Maria's experience, regarding this painful incident that she underwent due to her chemotherapy, had its positive aspect, too. It enabled the Society's spiritual healers to experience the effectiveness of spiritual healing in this field, allowing them to offer their help to other patients whenever they were about to undergo chemotherapy. Since then, these patients notify their healers of the day of their therapy and the healers work from afar, bringing them into their thoughts in the same way that I worked for Maria or in other ways, depending on the case. It has been proven from our experience that this assistance greatly reduces the side effects or even eliminates them altogether. But, even if some discomforts persist, the spiritual healing that is performed on the patients contributes to their calmness, making their discomforts less painful. This helps both them and their home environment, making it easier for them to cope with the whole unpleasant ordeal.

THE SOCIETY'S
HEALING SECTION

Spiritual healing, as I had predicted when I was first introduced to it, now played a dominant role in my life. My mental inclination to deal with and help people that were suffering grew on a daily basis, as the various forms of disharmony multiplied around me, besieging me in a way I could not ignore. Meanwhile, the number of patients I had healed kept increasing.

As time went by, I gained a greater awareness of what spiritual healing and spiritual healer meant. And so I gained the healer's consciousness that is merged with the "Healer in diffusion", God, as the Master said. I tried to see God in every manifestation of life, gazing at everything as if gazing at one of His faces, healing wherever I was, in any activity I took part in, not only when I was working for the patients. Our Master had taught us that everything needed to be permeated by God's radiance and that the healer, as a conduit of spiritual radiance, is called to pass it on to everyone and everything.

I made use of my presence in whatever area, whoever might be present, functioning as a healer, helping them calm and giving them again another form of spiritual healing. At first, I found this very difficult. My initial reaction was usually negative, but, after some thought, it could sometimes – not always – turn positive. I saw the negative side of situations, the negative traits of people and remained there. As time passed, however, this was corrected. I learned to apply, to the extent, of course, which I could each time, the messages of the teaching I received from the Society. I learned to look at people with love, the love I could give from my own stage of development, and to understand when they were in need of help; to convey to them a current of tranquillity, to radiate and to "heal" them. I learned to observe myself in depth as well as to perform healing on myself, whenever I needed it.

When I was invited to a house, for example, and realised that the people there where in an antagonistic mood, ready to clash, as often happens, I radiated them with light and love from the heart. Gradually the atmosphere turned from electrified to peaceful, the people from nega-

tive became positive and smiled having found their hu-
mour again. If, while walking on the street, I ran into a
group of people squabbling, I stood there for a moment,
imagining all of them inside the light, until they all found
their good spirits again. I did the same for a grumpy taxi
driver who would calm down, or a tired trolley driver who
would start telling jokes, forgetting his fatigue. All these
changes of mood, which might not seem especially sig-
nificant, are actual healings, since they can prevent un-
pleasant developments, such as tensions and conflicts
that can often affect human health, too.

The zeal I had demonstrated in working to smooth un-
pleasant situations and the experience I had gained with
this action, as well as all the other healings I had per-
formed, contributed to my being requested to undertake
the Society's spiritual healing section. The organisation
of this section had for some time been the responsibility
of Mrs Klairi Lykiardopoulou, always under the Master's
guidance, whenever she needed it. As Mrs Klairi was the
Society's president, she was engaged in many activities,
so it was deemed that I should replace her, taking over
the healing section.

Naturally, this proposal gave me mixed emotions;
gratification for the responsibility given to me, but also
certain doubts as to how ready I was to accomplish such
a task. I knew, of course, that it had already been some

time since the beginning of my discipleship and that it was time to devote myself more to the vocation. I also knew that one of the principles taught by the Master was that the knowledge acquired by individuals while training on spirituality does not belong to them and they have no right to keep it for themselves. On the contrary, they have a duty and obligation to pass it on to others, provided of course that the latter are willing to accept it. From the beginning I had fully adopted this principle and I was often given the chance to apply it, either on those who came to the Society asking for information on spiritual healing or as a healer on those who had a physical or psychological problem. All this knowledge brought me to accept the proposal to take on the Society's healing section, since, after all, I knew that the Master would always help me in any problem I encountered and in any difficulty that might arise.

From the establishment of the healing section until the time I took over its organisation, certain changes had taken place that needed to be dealt with immediately. The Society's members requesting to become healers had multiplied and had to be divided into groups so that they could work more efficiently. They all underwent the same training process which the senior members had also undergone. At the same time a group was formed in which all healers participated, senior and new, where issues regarding the methods of spiritual healing where discussed. Later on I also took over the training of this group, conveying to the younger members all the teachings I had received and continued to receive from the Master.

As time went by and the number of patients grew, we realised that we had to organise the healing subsections more efficiently. There were patients who brought us their medical history or sent it with a relative and asked simply to have healings performed regularly on them. For these patients groups of healers worked "from a distance" whenever they met for their work at the Society, twice a week. The same healing was performed by the healers at their home for patients who their group had been tasked with helping. In this way, we sought to continuously monitor all of the patients for their quickest treatment.

There was another group of patients who could not come to the Society, but were in great need of personal contact with the healers. We tried to help these patients by going to their homes or to wherever they were hospitalised, whenever, of course, this was feasible by the healers, as they also had their own numerous family and professional obligations. These visits were always accompanied by a senior and recognised healer. The purpose of this visit was mainly to help the patient psychologically by the healer's presence, as "distant" healing is by all means just as effective as the healing done when healer and patient have personal contact and communication.

Finally, another group of patients consisted of those who would come to the Society for "contact" healing. As the demand for this healing constantly grew, a special section was created that worked systematically on regular days for these patients. Each time, two or three trainee healers took part in the "contact" healing section, receiving through it the knowledge needed for their training. As head of the healing section I attended all "contact" healings, going through some very interesting experiences with patients who trusted the rehabilitation of their health literally "in our hands". I say "literally" because "contact" healing is a form of healing that is performed mainly with the help of the hands.

Concerning the "contact" healing the Master writes in one of his books addressed to the healers: "I place my hand and the body vibrates, the soul pulsates... The healer must believe that he has no hands of his own. The healing hands are the hands of all beings, that is the hands of the Entity and the healer simply makes use of them."

Difficult concepts, but magnificent. In my opinion, they should be an invaluable legacy for spiritual healers all over the world, and certainly will be one day. The Society's healers constantly study them, along with all the teachings they receive, and try to function through them as best they can, while gradually progressing in their understanding and realisation.

The healing section's course continued and the Master's teaching consolidated the healers to their work even more. The courses were becoming more specific and included the study of diseases, as they were explained by Medical Science. This knowledge should exist, to the extent possible, for the best function of the healers. Along with all of these studies there was also systematic work on acquiring relevant experiences regarding the energies and powers existing within the human body. This data contributes to the work of the spiritual healers, helping them to understand the patient's problem and respond to it accordingly. The correlation of this particular knowledge with meditative experiences helps the healers to understand how greatly these experiences correspond to the particular elements of each disease. Thus, the saying that "what is inside also appears on the outside" is validated.

THE ENERGY BODY

During my course as a spiritual healer and especially since I took over the healing section, the importance of this particular knowledge for my proper function was constantly confirmed. I searched for this knowledge in relevant books and also received it from the Master himself, whom I addressed whenever I had a question. I slowly began to understand many of the symptoms that my patients exhibited and to comprehend how to better help them. I will now describe an example of "contact" healing that shows how much our knowledge on the function of energies helps on the accomplishment of our healing work.

Alice was a young girl that came at times to visit us at the Society without, however, showing any particular interest in the teaching. She discussed with the members, acquired information on the groups and the healing work, but had not yet decided to participate in it. Having been informed at the time of the newly formed "contact" healing group, she came late one night to the Society, after finishing her work, desperately pleading us to perform a healing on her. Her whole body was in pain and she was suffering horribly. The cause was undetermined, probably of a neural nature as I could determine from the few explanations that she initially gave me. I did not consider it necessary to have a broader conversation with her, which usually happens in most cases, as the need to relieve her of her pains as soon as possible was more important.

I would try to understand the reasons that caused them later. The other healers of the "contact" group had gone, since the last patient of the day had left. However, it was not possible to deny her the assistance she asked for and so I decided to perform the healing on my own.

I followed the well-known procedures for merging with the Entity and began giving instructions to Alice for a special relaxation exercise. This method sought to raise the awareness of her body's own cells so that she realised that within her whole body there is energy, life force. This awareness would help her spread the energy throughout her body and discharge the areas that hurt her so. Indeed, in a little while she had calmed down considerably. I then placed my hands above her head, imagining them as the hands of the Entity, and channelled light into all of her body, so as to relieve it of the pains, while also revitalising it at the same time.

It must have been two minutes when Alice started breathing with difficulty as if she could not inhale. I stopped and leaned forward to see what was happening. I had the knowledge and experience to understand that such events simply indicate that the treatment will be successful. And this knowledge was based on an analysis that the Master had made to spiritual healers. We had asked him once:

"How can we explain, Master, why a patient sometimes appears worse at the beginning of a spiritual healing?"

"When healing is performed on a patient," he replied, "the energies within are forced to move in a way not used to by the body of the patient, thus reactions are formed. These energies are either idle or malfunctioning and spiritual healing puts them in motion and in their proper function. This upsets the sustained energies which are like stagnant water, and briefly creates discomfort and unpleasant symptoms in the body, which quickly pass, usually giving way to a course of gradual improvement."

So, having this knowledge, I was not worried about Alice's symptoms. It was natural, however, for her to worry, and so I had to do something to calm her down. I followed the inner prompting that came to me at that time and placed my hand on her abdominal area, visualising the healing power concentrating within my hand and passing on to the solar plexus, where it dissolved the accumulated emotions. Soon Alice's breathing had settled. On any patient on whom healing is performed and regardless of what condition he or she is suffering from, an attempt to calm the solar plexus is always useful. Patients, no matter how calm they might seem, surely have fears and concerns about their situation and the outcome of their disease. Therefore, a healing to the solar plexus calms the negative emotions and relieves them.

When I realised that Alice had calmed down I asked her if she felt any pain and in which part of her body.

"On the neck," she replied.

I placed both my open palms near her neck. I felt them vibrating and warming up from the energy accumulated there. With the healing it dissolved and spread outwards, releasing the neck. The pain passed but suddenly her ears hurt. I moved the conduits of spiritual power – my hands – in front of her ears and again felt the same vibration and heat from the accumulated energy in them. The same happened shortly after in her meninges too and then at the top of her head and then on her neck again and then behind her ears. Alice would indicate it to me and I would rush to help dissolve it. Finally, at some point the pain stopped completely. I knew, however, that this "game" inside Alice's head could start again, so I kept going for a while longer.

My connection to the healing power continued. I had a strong sense of its presence near me, guiding me when I needed it. I felt that I had to work again on Alice's solar plexus and after a while on her heart. As soon as I did, I suddenly felt that her chest was disrupted and her breathing became erratic again. I looked at her and saw that she wanted to cry, but she would not let it be seen, obviously because she was afraid I would consider her weak and dismiss her. I then told her to open herself up to whatever came to her and to be happy, as I was, because her tendency to cry showed that the healing had released the energies trapped in her solar plexus and her heart.

"Cry! Let yourself free! Do not be afraid to show what you feel," I told her. And, indeed, Alice let herself cry.

The healing in these two areas of her body, her heart and solar plexus, manifested with a pain between the shoulder blades, a reflection of the point which was actually ailing, her "heart". I sensed that she needed a warm embrace and so I radiated her with love and mentally embraced her. As the Master says, "the patient must be embraced through the healer's arms and the healer must regard these arms as the arms of nature, the arms of the world, the arms of God."

I realised that the few tears still running from Alice's eyes where tears of emotion and gratitude for the help she had received and the improvement of her situation.

"Thank you, thank you!" she kept repeating. Her face had taken on a sweet expression and I was sure that the feeling of mergence that had been built, as is always built, between the Entity and the spiritual healer, poured into her, as it did into me, the blessing of the Divine Grace which I had channelled to her as a conduit. Without realising what was happening to her, though I did as I had the relevant knowledge, she seemed to feel to some extent the rejoicing of this mergence with the Divine, as I felt it too.

Alice's healing had to be repeated a few more times in order to be complete and had to include a mental process, too, a dialogue between us which would bring the true cause of her suffering to surface. Only then could we say that we had offered her essential assistance, on the necessary condition that she would also decide to work consciously on it. But Alice did not make that decision. She came to the Society one more time and I performed a healing on her again, which did not have the same difficulties and pains, as there were no longer any tensions, and we had an initial discussion regarding her problems. From then on she stopped seeking the help of spiritual healing and only occasionally appeared at the Society for a simple contact with its members.

It is possible that Alice simply settled on an observation by medical science, as we had recommended her to do, and as we do whenever it is needed by the patients seeking help from us. What primarily interests us is that the patients are relieved from the ordeal of their disease by following any treatment that suits them. We are, of course, mainly interested in the consolidation of spirituality within them, in the realisation of the omnipresence of God which is the only treatment for everything and everyone. This, however, can only happen with the will of the human being and his or her decision to overcome the resistances of their personality.

Before concluding this chapter, I will make a brief reference to the human energy field, as described by scholars of the subject, which will help the reader better understand the work of the healer as well as the problems that appear within its duration, as happened during Alice's healing. Most diseases are caused by the unconscious inhibition of energy flow within the body and that is why the healer works through the energy body to restore the patient's health. This field is part of the uniform energy that exists within all of Creation, the cosmic energy, which is also present and flowing through all forms and even in the amorphous spaces between them, thereby connecting all physical bodies of the universal world.

Inside the human being the cosmic energy receives

from birth three basic forms of manifestation, the so called energy bodies: the etheric, the emotional or astral and the mental. The etheric body is what feeds the physical form with vitality and is present everywhere, in the cells, in the organs, throughout the entire body. It is identical to the physical body and extends beyond it to a distance of around five to ten centimetres, forming a kind of radiance around it. The emotional body is the sum of all the emotions and the mental body is the sum of all human mental functions.

The energy inside the human is allocated to individual energies necessary for life and the growth of his or her consciousness. For this to happen it passes through seven main focus points, also called energy centres, all positioned along the spine, except for one which is above the head. Each centre is responsible for the function of the part of the physical body in which it is located, as well as the corresponding function of the soul.

For example, the centre of the "heart" is responsible for the organ of the heart and the entire thorax, but also for the expression of love. The centre of the "solar plexus" is responsible for the abdominal area with all the organs it contains, but also for the function of emotions.

Starting from top to bottom, the first is the centre of the "head" with its focal point outside of the head, which connects the human being to the cosmic energy, merging him or her with cosmic consciousness. Following that is the "third eye" on the forehead, which develops distinction, then we have the centre of the neck, whose proper activation increases knowledge, and the centre of the heart whose goal is the development of love, as we have already said. The rest of the centres are below the diaphragm with first the solar plexus in the abdominal area, then the centre of the "genitals" on a point above the spline which, through the sensual satisfaction it provides, leads to the covering of instinctive functions, and, lastly, the centre of the "base" on the lower end of the spine, where the energy is grounded before returning upwards again.

A requirement for the health of the human being is the equal distribution of energy to all energy centres and its seamless flow from one to the other. When the flow is halted and one centre is charged, the symptoms of disease begin. The spiritual healer works to dissolve the detentions and that is why spiritual healing is performed on the area of the energy body without the need for hand contact with the physical body. The correct flow of energy then helps in the treatment of physical disease.

Much more can be said about the energy body but this subject can be studied by whoever is interested with the relevant books. What is important for the work of spiritual healing is for the healers to be able to mentally bond with the patient and to experience for themselves the flow of energy in their body and to then pass it on with no inhibitions to the one seeking help. Knowledge essentially helps only when it becomes experience and when the healer takes a genuine interest in the patient.

THE FEAR OF CHANGE

"Take a sponge and erase everything you know!" I heard the voice of my conscience telling me one day while I was in deep meditation, at the beginning of my discipleship. I was startled at the time, considering this declaration excessive. To erase everything that I know? And what will then be left? Who will I be?

These words were urging me to forget everything, if I really desired to be a disciple of spirituality. They encouraged me to completely change my life, my way of thinking, my habits. It was not an easy job! Although I soon realised their catalysing importance, there were many changes that needed to be made, and, therefore, many sacrifices were required. My decision for change was consolidated with my discipleship and with the ascertainment that every sacrifice leads to redemption. As I processed this issue I saw that there were people not willing to undergo sacrifices. Even when they realise that their sacrifices are life-saving and beneficial to their lives they often prefer to resign, abandoning the effort.

In the Society we often deal with this phenomenon; for people, in other words, to withdraw even though they see that they are helped by discipleship and spiritual healing and that their situation is improving. The explanation of this phenomenon is found, of course, in one basic cause; the flight from effort and the changes it requires. This cause is, however, manifested in many different aspects in which it is also contained and which cause the flight without, most times, realising its true motive.

Individuals might, for example, be frightened by the power of spiritual healing which they feel spreading within them, relieving them of pain or reducing psychological stress. Or they may, without realising it, not want to actually be deprived of this pain and stress even though they have come to the Society for this reason, requesting it of us. In such a case it is obvious that they have not realised that deep down they are attached to the conditions they believe they want to eliminate. They cannot see that this attachment creates a framework of security and intimacy through which they are accustomed to function, feeling comfortable simply because it is familiar to them. Even if it is something annoying and unpleasant, such as a pain, they may unconsciously strive to keep it, so that they do not have to undergo change which is unknown and frightening to them. And change might cause them fear – without them consciously realising it – because changing means the end of a condition, a small death. And all small deaths eventually lead to the great death, the death of form, the end of its life.

In my course as a spiritual healer I have met people that discontinue their healing out of fear, conscious or unconscious. Of all of these cases I will now recount the one I consider the most characteristic:

Marianna was an acquaintance of mine, about forty-five years old, with whom I found myself in the country-side one summer. Every time we met, we chatted about our favourite subjects; the Society, its teaching and spiritual healing. She really liked everything she heard and seemed ready to accept them, as I perceived from her questions and the interest she showed.

One day she told me about her neck pains that had been bothering her daily for years and the various therapeutic methods she had occasionally followed to no avail. In her own way she made me understand that she was burning from desire to try out spiritual healing. She was, however, very indecisive and hesitant to suggest it to me, perhaps because she did not really believe in it, despite all of our discussions. Although I really wanted to help her, I deemed it advisable not to make the initial suggestion myself. I knew that people feel pressured when you offer a service against their will and should feel free to decide on their own when and if to ask for it. My own past experiences had taught me this attitude towards others regarding issues relating to the teaching and spiritual healing. A few days had passed since our first discussion about Marianna's problem when she finally broke her silence and openly asked if I could help in diminishing her pains by performing spiritual healing.

I proceeded to invite her to my home one afternoon, picking a quiet room where no one would disturb us and where she would feel comfortable, and had her sit down. I gave her an initial relaxation, calming her down, and then invoked the help of the Almighty for the healing. My palms near her neck began to heat up more and more and reached the point of burning, discharging the area of its accumulated energy.

To facilitate the process I visualised all charges scattering around me in the form of sparks. I could see through my inner vision that that was indeed the case as I constantly felt the excess heat that was being drawn into my hands and dispersing. This feeling was very intense and lively, revealing Marianna's positive response to spiritual healing. It showed, as we say, that she was "open", allowing the healing power to freely direct the confined energies outwards.

I continued working merged with the Higher Self, pleading Him to guide me in His work and show me when to stop the healing. Suddenly, as I was immersed, focused on my inner work, I felt Marianna's body suddenly spring upright in front of me. Just as I opened my eyes I saw her practically running out of the room without uttering a single word. It was obvious that something had upset her, but instead of waiting for the healing to finish and then discuss what had bothered her, she decided she could not stand it and ran, alarmed, as if to escape a dangerous enemy.

When we met the next day, I asked her to explain to me what had made her run and she described everything as she had experienced it. The heat on her neck was very intense on her as it was on my hands, too. But while I knew what it meant and welcomed its existence, Marianna did not and got very scared. Moreover, my mental work on visualising the dispersal of the accumulated energy – which was in fact happening – spread the feeling of warmth throughout her body. That resulted in her feeling a living liquid flowing and passing through her without, however, knowing what it was. The worst thing, as she told me, was the tightness caused in her heart. What had alarmed her and had scared her most of all was something quite simple and harmless.

Marianna is a rather "closed" person, by no means effusive. This closure is usually due to fears and insecurities that hinder the proper functioning of the energy centre of the heart, thus limiting the expression of love. With the power of spiritual healing that raises the energy flow through the body, the centre of the heart also vibrates, expanding and functioning better. Until, however, this expansion takes place, an accumulation of energy might form there, a blockage and a pressure resulting in a tightness such as the one that frightened Marianna. This soon disappears if the patient calmly waits for the continuation of the healing, which, of course, requires confidence in this vocation.

Marianna's attitude revealed that she didn't trust spiritual healing, having been only superficially affected by our long conversations about it. Had she waited with patience and faith in God to finish she wouldn't have been frightened at all. On the contrary, she would have been left with the pleasant realisation that her situation had considerably improved. As she stated on this second meeting she had felt very well after calming down from her initial reaction. However, the decrease in pain didn't convince her to continue the healing work, as I suggested to her. Thus, she deprived herself of an essential aid that could have possibly lead to the complete cure of her condition.

Mrs Klairi refers to the issue of fear and the deeper reasons that cause it in a chapter of her book "Master IV-Realisation, Spiritual Healing." I convey here excerpts from this chapter in which an analysis by the Master is included. Klairi Lykiardopoulou says:

"Often the question arises of whether fear on the human level is only a derivative of instinct or if it is associated with emotions and thoughts. There is a view that because of their complex nature the feeling that humans feel is not pure fear but an equally complex reaction to anything threatening them. Insecurity, stress, agony, depression, obsessions, ideas, phobias are the negative experiences of humanity, experiences indeed much more complex than the intuitive function of the animal. We could say, however, that they all have their source in the same original fear and the same cause, the need for self-protection. A need which on the human field is not only limited to the sustenance of the body and the avoidance of deterioration and death, but also extends to all levels of existence. Humans are scared of oppression, rejection, loneliness, failure, abandonment. They are even afraid of the externalisation of themselves, of any action, when they believe that it can expose their ego to real or imaginary dangers. The fear for the loss of form increases with the addition of the fear for the loss of personality or even its reduction from something that could affect it, hurt it, cause it pain.

There is also a deeper purpose for the existence of fear and that is to lead humans, through the problems they create, in search of the path to fearlessness, to strength, to certainty, to calmness. As many psychiatrists note, fear and its unpleasant consequences should not be perceived as enemies, but, instead, should be treated as motives that lead to alertness and positive action."

And Mrs Klairi continues: "Referring to this issue, the Master says: 'Everything in the world – and by saying everything, we mean all beings but particularly humans – are governed by fear, the great benefactor. This is a responsibility of the Entity, in order for humans to learn the nature of this fear; because the nature of every fear is the nature of humans and the nature of humans is nothing but the nature of God, in other words the nature of the Entity itself. However, it is a nature reversed by humans; Phoebus* (light-knowledge) has become Phobos (darkness-ignorance). Humans fear what they do not know and what they do not really want to know is God, who is inside them and inside everything and who is unconsciously also themselves.'"

---

* Editor's note: "Phoebus" was another name for the ancient Greek god Apollo, literally meaning "bright", commonly used by the Greeks in Apollo's role as the god of light. "Phobos" is the personification of fear in Greek mythology.

DENIAL OF HEALING

Aside from the reasons we saw in the previous chapter that are responsible for the interruption of a healing from the patient's side – fear of change and death, an unconscious need to maintain pain due to insecurity, clinging to tension etc. – there are also several other reasons. In these cases the denial towards spiritual healing may be due to a person's ignorance of its actual significance or it may be the result of various circumstances in life, specific to each person, such as childhood, negative family environments and others still. The examples I describe below speak for themselves.

John, who was eleven years old, came one afternoon to the Society along with his mother. His ears had been bothering him, aching and leaking fluids. His mother, who was a person with spiritual concerns and quests, had heard of the spiritual healing performed at the Society and wanted to be informed about it and find out if her child's ears could be healed. She had already sought a solution in medicine without any positive results up to then.

At first I talked to her a bit, giving her a general idea of what spiritual healing is and how it functions so that she could trust her son to it. I emphasized to her that spiritual healers do not promise anything, as they cannot know in advance how things will turn out for each patient, what his or her responsiveness will be and above all what the will of the Almighty will be concerning the healing. I also told her that healers are always willing to work on any case with the wish and hope that the abilities of spiritual healing will perform to their fullest for a positive healing result.

I proceeded to lead John to a quiet room in the Society, and, after following the initial familiar procedures, I placed my palms in front of his ears and mentally "wrapped" them in light, thus creating the necessary communication between us, between the "ill" and the spiritual healer. When I felt my palms vibrate, I realised that John was a positive receiver of spiritual healing. I continued to work visualising that, as I became a conduit of divine power, the high level with which I was consciously merged passed to him internally, touching the strings of his soul. He was not, of course, consciously aware of this communication, but his soul certainly experienced and responded to it. The healing of that day was concluded when the vibration in my palms started decreasing and eventually completely faded.

John and his mother came back another three times and I worked with him in the same way. There was still quite a bit of tension in his ears, as the energies that temporarily left with the healing later gathered again to a degree bringing with them the initial symptoms. It was a case that would need a few iterations of the healing work to be completed. But John was tired, he got bored, lost his patience, probably because of his young age, and, one afternoon, during the healing and towards its end, got up from his chair and left the room stating to his mother that he did not want to continue. His ears were eventually cured with the help of science. As for his mother, she soon became a member of the Society and has since been attending its courses regularly without fail.

John's attitude was similar to that of a girl called Anna, whom we considered a unique case among those that have gone through the "contact" healing section, unique in regard to her reaction. She suffered from stomach ulcers that had also unsettled her mental equilibrium. We performed "distant" healing on her for a while and regularly monitored her course.

Anna had separated from her husband and this had overturned her life, causing this ailment. She lived with her young daughter and her mother, who believed that she was helping her by being overprotective and restrictive. One of the things she had forbidden was spiritual healing, of which they heard of from an acquaintance of theirs who happened to be one of our patients and was actually doing very well. Anna's mother refused to allow us to heal her daughter. She, however, wanted to try, so, ignoring her mother's refusal, brought us her medical data. As was natural there was constant friction between mother and daughter concerning this matter. The daughter, as a patient with a weakened resolve, tried not to let it affect her negatively, but did not succeed. She gradually lost her faith in spiritual healing, as she was not able to get to know it and acquire her own perspective on it.

One day Anna came to the Society and reluctantly climbed the staircase leading to the healing area. I came out to greet her, knowing of her difficulties and indecision. She did not want to enter the room. I spoke to her with love and understanding, trying to reassure her and convey calmness and confidence to her, but to no avail. Anna, like a terrified and defenceless animal trying to escape an unseen danger, firmly refused and descended the stairs to leave and never come back again. Her mother's reaction had won.

After her absolute resistance, which was not really hers, but a reflection of her mother's ideas, we also ceased the "distant" healing we had been performing on her. The patient must have no resistance to spiritual healing, but to willingly accept it, eager to test its abilities. That is the reason why healers always ask for their patients' written consent before starting their healing work.

There is also another category of patients, rarer – truth be told – who do not externalise any denial for spiritual healing, since they themselves have requested its aid. This denial, that the patients themselves seem to not be aware of, is perceived through an internal process, in other words through the spiritual healer's healing meditation.

A group of healers went through this kind of experience while they were working on a patient suffering from Parkinson's disease. Every healer in one's own different way, with different symbols and experiences, had the same revelations that lead to one conclusion: this patient did not want to be healed. I convey here the words and impressions of one of the healers of that group referring to this particular case:

"While I meditated on the patient I began to feel a resistance that constantly grew until it reached a clear denial in accepting the healing. I tried to pass on to him my feelings of completeness so as to calm him down but I felt that he continued to resist. I eventually stopped this effort limiting myself to simply enlightening him for a while until I finally discontinued my meditative work."

We were seriously troubled by this denial. We wanted our decision on continuing or discontinuing the healing to be truly in line with the patient's will and not the result of our own, possibly incorrect, impression, which could lead us on the wrong path. We also wanted to know if the denial we were internally experiencing was the denial of his soul or just the denial of his personality, of his personal ego. We asked the advice of the Master, to avoid any error, and he said the following:

"The true nature of a patient's or of any other person's soul seeks spiritual healing, seeks in other words its mergence with the Source, with God. What reacts to a varying degree of intensity is the personality. When the soul is not yet strong enough to lead the personality on its own course, then the personality lures the soul, something that causes difficulties in accepting spiritual healing.

The healers must persist in their efforts to help the soul. This will eventually bring the results, thus also helping the patient's body. Only when the patients themselves request the discontinuation of their healing for their own reasons or when they stop meeting their obligation towards the healing section of informing it regularly on the state of their health, only then do we stop our work. And, of course, we are aware that this is again the personality's reaction, not the soul's."

Following the Master's advice we continued the healing of this patient who suffered from Parkinson's disease. After two or three days, however, we received a message from his family to stop the healing, as he did not wish to continue. And so the same element of denial of healing and the patient's choice to not receive help was given in the physical field, as well as the internal. We had no doubts left that we had to stop our work, according to the Master's words, and so we did. As we were later informed from one of the patient's acquaintances, his situation did not improve because his general attitude towards life was very negative, as it had also been towards spiritual healing.

As the denial of healing affects negatively, so does receptiveness affect positively, helping to improve health. At the same time that the above incident took place, a healing was being performed by the same group of healers on another patient who also had Parkinson's disease. She, however, offered no resistance on accepting it, something that was mentally affirmed by all of the group's healers and as a result her condition constantly improved. I mention this case to illustrate the importance of the patient's responsiveness to the healing and the results that follow as a natural consequence of the positive or negative way of dealing with it. The healers are aware of this importance and always request God's aid for the change of the patients' attitude towards His healing work, whenever it is negative, so that they stop resisting and accept His help.

HEALING WITH THE ACTIVE PARTICIPATION OF THE PATIENT

Sometimes a spiritual healer happens to receive a call from a patient asking to immediately intervene in order to address an urgent health problem. This work is a form of healing that seldom occurs among the incidents of the Society's healing section as the patients that can be helped by it must possess certain knowledge concerning meditation and the human energy body.

Up to now the readers of this book have encountered two types of healing, "contact" and "distant". Here, however, we have something different. This is neither a "contact" healing, as healer and patient are not close by, nor is it "distant", as they might be at a distance from each other but they still have an essential communication between them; the patient is "present" at the healing, following the healer's instructions. He or she participates in the work of the healing and accordingly contributes to its success as a patient.

In the following lines I will describe an incident that will clearly show the similarities and differences between these three healing methods. For example, the difference of this healing from the one performed in Maria's case with the chemotherapy side effects described in Chapter IV, will be obvious. That was a «remote» healing as, although I had made use of the telephone, its use was very brief and without the patient's participation to the healing. The patient merely announced her case to the healer, invoking the protection of the spiritual power.

The healing that follows was performed on a member of the Society who was bothered from palpitation attacks. These attacks made her feel as though she flared up and faded at the same time, completely losing contact with life, feeling as if she was dying. As a disciple of the Society she was trained to deal with her problem by performing healing on herself, but, sometimes, no healing regimen and no effort of hers could calm her down. She consequently needed the intervention of someone else who would be able to relieve her of this ordeal.

Katie was bothered from various phobias, which, whenever they overwhelmed her, immobilised her for a certain period of time, sometimes smaller and sometimes greater, causing these attacks. She was being healed by the Society's healing section as well as by her doctor with the appropriate medications. Her spiritual healers had carried out a number of discussions with her, aiding her in realising several causes of her phobias. Yet she still had not been healed. It seems there were certain traumatic experiences that insisted in hiding within her unconscious, refusing to come to light, so that Katie could see them and be permanently relieved of them.

The explanation that was given was that Katie's personality, her ego, did not want to lose what it gained every time her attack manifested; the care of those close to her, the preoccupation of others with her, their express of love and concern. That is why it caused the attacks. In this way, a vicious circle was formed that could not be easily broken. Katie's ego acquired the satisfaction it demanded but the phobias that had caused this attack as well as the rest of the negative feelings that accompanied it, such as agony, disappointment, and guilt, energetically charged her solar plexus. The result of this charge was the weakening of the brain and an inadequately functioning mind due to the lack of necessary energies that were trapped predominantly in her solar plexus. Thus, Katie could not "mentally face", as we say, her problem, she could not, in other words, think calmly and clearly, remaining at the mercy of her feelings. And so the attack ran its course.

What would save Katie whenever she suffered an attack would be a clear mind with healthy thoughts that would dominate over the solar plexus, making her emotions calm down. Furthermore, a clear mind would influence her ego with its logic, cancelling the need for this attack to supposedly gain the care of her loved ones and feel secure, since, after all, she was the only one doubting their love and care for her.

I made this analysis of Katie's case for two reasons. Firstly, because it will help the reader in understanding the healing method I followed and, secondly, because her problem is quite common. And this problem is the accumulation of energy in a centre – usually the solar plexus – thus weakening other centres, making their proper function correspondingly difficult. When the spiritual healers know the patients' energy problem, they can help them more directly, working for the discharge of the centre retaining the energy and restoring the proper flow to all of the other centres.

When Katie called me, her voice was so distorted from agony that I had trouble recognising her. I was startled and lost it for a moment, but I soon regained my composure, focusing on the need presented to me and to which I had to respond without delay. As I knew of her situation I immediately realised what I had do to help her.

After saying a few reassuring words to her I asked her to sit down somewhere and make herself comfortable. I was aware that she herself wished to participate in the healing and so I kept her on the phone, giving her verbal instructions and guidance.

Since Katie's solar plexus was agitated, she could not partake in the healing work. She had to relax first and then proceed to the main part of the healing. Besides, relaxation was itself a part of the work. I explained my thinking to her, revealing my main objective to her, the strengthening of her mind and the control of her emotions. I then told her to send light to her abdominal area and visualise the energies there discharging and heading towards the brain.

This alone could be a healing for the patient, as what she needed was basically the tranquillity that always comes with the proper flow of energy throughout the entire body. Katie responded to some extent to the instructions I was giving to her and her breathing calmed. Soon, however, the palpitation began again, because, as she said, a new fear had overwhelmed her. This continued for a few minutes until I decided to give her a different healing regimen, believing that it would help her more. Katie had been receiving the teaching for some time, and, therefore, was able to understand and use it on her healing.

This regimen aims at the realisation of the mergence that exists on the spiritual level between healer and patient. It concerns the spiritual nature of human beings, which is the divine essence within them, the Spirit of God. The realisation of the spiritual nature of all human beings and the inner mergence that exists between them leads to completeness, to tranquillity, to bliss.

As I guided Katie on visualising that we are merged "in God", I asked her at times how she felt, in a low voice, so as not to disturb the tranquillity that had prevailed from the moment I spoke to her of her spiritual nature. She would answer me in the same tone, saying that she felt a deep reverence, the same that I felt, too, the reverence that every human feels when communicating with the Spirit, with the Entity, with God. That is why the Master says that the "spiritual healer, while performing spiritual healing, heals and is healed", because the mergence with the Spirit, with which the healer consciously communicates, is the only true healing.

I continued Katie's healing for a little while longer until it was complete. I asked her how she felt and she said that the palpitation attack had stopped and that she felt great serenity. This time she had made an essential step towards the definitive cure of her condition. She had also realised what happened to her each time she had an attack. Lastly, she had observed, to the extent that she was able to, the movement of the energies through her body and its results. She had felt the discharge of her solar plexus – the fear, agony and panic had left – and the strengthening of the brain's function – her thoughts had calmed down and she was made aware of her condition.

Today the attacks have been reduced to a minimum in frequency and intensity and Katie now has control of herself and overcomes the palpitation tendency which might sometimes be about to occur. The healing, as well as the regular following of the teaching that guides her to the recognition of her spiritual nature and her mergence with it, contributed to this.

This incident of healing "by phone" is not the only one. Other healers have reported similar experiences. The common feature between all of them is the involvement of the patients in the healing work and their constant communication with the healers who guide them on what they must do. The healing techniques used by the healers talking to the patients vary depending on the case, the patients' knowledge and their ability to respond. All, however, have the common goal of relieving them of their problem, as is also the case with "contact" and "distant" healings.

THE EFFECT OF SPIRITUAL
HEALING ON THE HEALER

There is a view regarding spiritual healers' fatigue claiming that they tire with the healing work because they absorb the negative state of their patients. They absorb the pain, the disease or simply the tension, as they work to relieve their patients. At the same time, because they play the part of the conduit between the Entity and the "ill" to whom they convey positive powers, this view advocates that healers need a certain amount of time between two consecutive healings, as it is believed that they are "drained" and weakened so that the other person can "fill up", strengthening by receiving these powers. Healers, therefore, need this time to regain their "lost" strength while also releasing themselves of the negative state brought upon them by the healing.

The Society's teaching has a different approach on this subject and its truth is validated daily by its healers. The conductivity of the spiritual healer is not limited to conveying spiritual power to the patients, but continues until the patients place their troubles on the Entity and are freed of them. The purpose of spiritual healing is for patient and healer to both be healthy. This is achieved by the continuous flow of energy from the healer's body to the patient's body and not by its retention by the healer. It is also achieved when both of them feel strong and not when the healer feels tired and weak after the healing.

When the healers are in the proper state of a conduit and not of one that heals individually, when they are in a state of strength and faith on the one hand and true humility on the other, then they keep nothing for themselves. They do not keep the bright beneficial energy that the Entity directs towards the patient as they are very much aware of its destination and the purpose of its existence. They know very well the sanctity of their own part as a conduit of the divine power, and would never consider appropriating it. This power, however, the healing power and the love of God, when passing through them, heading towards the patient, also strengthens the healers, too, working to cleanse their 'vehicles' of any negative elements that might have existed before the healing work.

Apart from the spiritual power that flows through the healers, there is also the retained energy that emanates from the patients, dispelling the unpleasant state of their condition. The healers do not retain this energy, but, as a conduit, let it flow towards the Entity, the only true healer of all. This is the training that healers receive at the Society and that is why they do not feel any tiredness, nor do they feel as though they have absorbed the condition leaving the patient. It is possible that they might become charged for a while, or it is possible that during the course of the healing they might feel warm or sweaty or even feel a trace of pain, similar to the patient's whom they are aiding. Soon, however, these symptoms all flee, leaving them cleansed and rejuvenated, even stronger than they were before the healing process began. Spiritual healing never creates problems for the healers. These are only created because of their own ignorance or selfish function.

During the period I was training as a spiritual healer, I too had an unpleasant experience while performing a healing. The patient I was working for had a cyst in her internal genitals. While I was trying to make the cyst dissolve and disappear during a "contact" healing, I suddenly felt an intense pain in my own body at the same place as the patient's. I was alarmed, as I was not yet established as a healer and lost my faith at every opportunity, doubting and questioning. I ended the healing, apologising to the patient, and ran to the Master to report the incident.

"Do not be afraid, Mrs Kiki," he told me, "it is nothing. It seems that you had a very strong desire to succeed in the healing, incorporating selfishness in your work. Calm down, assume the correct state of offering and everything will pass."

At once I realised what had really happened and so I proceeded to do as he told me. I had charged the work I was doing for the patient with overzealousness, wanting to heal through my ego and not through true love and the function of the soul. Unconsciously of course, this desire made me retain the power that I should be conveying to the patient's body, and so, instead of letting it flow, I accumulated it in my body, feeling the same symptom as her. Once I realised what I had done the tension left, taking with it all pain and worries. I ran back to the patient lightened and reassured, and continued the healing without the overzealousness that had caused my error.

Healers might feel similar unpleasant symptoms if, for personal reasons, they have a negative reaction to a disease, a pain, or a fatigue. They might then briefly identify with the symptom bothering them, feeling it in their own body. If, however, they realise what is happening to them then they will quickly overcome their personal resistances and continue the healing, rested and strong. The fatigue of spiritual healers is a myth for anyone that is in the correct state of mergence with God and not the identification with their ego, their human weaknesses and negative thoughts. The appeal for mergence with the Higher Self, with the level of the soul, exists in all people, it is an unconscious need which they are not aware of if they do not have the relevant education. Healers are trained to consciously pass into this mergence as they work with the patients. The Master says:

"I practice spiritual healing literally means that I practice the energies and powers of the soul, I willingly practice the Soul's inclination – not 'my soul's inclination' but the Soul's inclination generally. For the Soul is one, and it is no other than the right visualization in the form of complete emotions that stem from selfless thoughts. They, also, stem from the complete lack of ego and not from its projection, stated by utterances like 'I am a healer', 'I perform spiritual healing' etc. Soul is the absolute interest – in the form of duty – in the work we have undertaken that is spiritual healing.

The spiritual inclination of all people and, of course, patients to be merged with God considerably helps the work of the healers when they consciously work on aiding the patients on this mergence. This fact has been known since ancient times and is demonstrated by the healings performed in ancient Greece, as mentioned by the Master in one of his books on spiritual healers. At the Asclepieia* there were priests who functioned as healers, and who, knowing of their patient's needs, treated their soul in the appropriate way in order to heal them. In other words they guided their souls to a treatment – psychagogia** – that aimed to liberate the powers and energies of the soul achieving the mergence with the Entity, with Its healing power. The success of the healing depended on the faith of the patients, their spiritual inclination and their trust towards the priests. In current times, the behaviour of the healer regarding the practice of psychagogia**, cannot be the same, at least concerning the rites and performances. It must, however, be the same, as the Master says, regarding the essence of the spiritual relationship between healers and patients. They must inspire trust and love in them in order to help express their spiritual inclination for mergence.

In relation to the above, I would like to mention the case of a patient suffering from spondylarthritis, because I consider her first experience of "contact" healing very important. She lived far from Athens and up to then had received only "distant" healing. She occasionally received

---

* In ancient Greece an Asclepieion (plural: Asclepieia) was a healing temple, sacred to the god of medicine and healing Asclepius.
** Literally meaning "leading the soul".

other treatments, too, just like many other patients, who, while seeking help from the Society, also resort to other therapeutic methods at the same time.

When the spiritual healing with us was concluded that day, her physiognomy had completely changed, she had sweetened remarkably, having a serene expression that revealed her soul's matching mood. Without us asking how she felt, she told us of the religious reverence she had felt and of the piety that came with the exercise of spiritual healing. She then spoke to us for the first time of the other treatment she had been having at the same time with spiritual healing, just to mention the difference between the two. In the other treatment there was no sense of the divine or holy and the patient had never thought that she might possibly experience such a sensation after a healing effort. The different experience from spiritual healing was due to the healers' spiritual embrace and their constant reference to God, which she experienced internally even though she was unaware of it consciously.

The Master says that what is missing from the healers of many healing methods is the awareness of the mergence between the patient with themselves – the healers – and the Entity. There is no consciousness of the fact that the spiritual healer is in reality every healer and every doctor and that spiritual healing is every healing.

The Master says:

"Spiritual healing is a constant hymn of a timeless praise to God and that is how spiritual healers should regard it. They monitor and work, work and participate, participate as a mind observer and as a supplier of power, of radiance, of love, of spirituality.»

According to this analysis, is it ever possible for a spiritual healer to tire? Is it possible for me to be tired by performing healing on the woman with the cyst or the woman with spondylarthritis? And is it possible that I held inside of me for more than a few minutes the pain from the cyst when my only concern was to convey to her body the energy of the healing and the love of God? This love gives me strength and health, too, healing me whenever I need it, as it does for all healers. This has been proven many times, when, at the end of a healing work, the healers realise that they are also relieved of an annoyance, a headache, a cold, etc. And even more serious problems are healed without the healers dealing with them, as they immediately or after a while realise that they are completely well. The example I describe below is indicative of the healing power's function, as described by a healer:

"When I became a member of the Society's spiritual healing group, I had been suffering from chronic bronchial asthma. This had started three years before and had such intensity that I had to use an inhaler four to six times a day to calm down. If there was a high level of humidity I used it up to eight times a day.

With the regular practice of healing on patients, and without performing any healing work on myself or following any medication, I became completely well. Along with my asthma, a spring allergy that had been bothering me since I was in the first grades of elementary school also disappeared.

Considering the subject, I realised that I had also been healed of the constant emotional charge I previously had and which was the cause of my problems. And this happened with the help of the healing power that ran through my body, to be channelled to the patients."

This example, along with many others, confirms the words of the Master: "The spiritual healer, by the act of healing, is healed!"

SELF-HEALING

The training that spiritual healers receive in the Society includes the healing they must perform on themselves whenever needed. Although they are essentially helped by healing others, there are times when they have to focus on a personal health issue, sometimes an easy case and sometimes a difficult one. I will convey here certain self-healing examples as described to me by the healers.

Antigone has been a member of the Society for several years and in fact today she is in charge of one of the groups of novice healers. Since the beginning of her discipleship she had shown a spiritual inclination towards healing work, as shown by the stability displayed in a healing that she performed on herself, of which she says the following:

"For years I have been bothered by colitis and constipation which have greatly discomforted me. When I learned to relax and become aware of the energies within my body, I decided to perform self-healing. I started working daily, visualising a bright light bathing my entire being. I focused mainly on the area of my abdomen and bowels. Sometimes I felt as though there was within me a bright waterfall cleansing me of the pain and sometimes I felt as though the bowels moved assuming their correct position. At the end of each relaxation I experienced a great relief, my abdomen deflated and the pain subsided.

This sensation lasted a few hours and then the discomforts began again. I repeated this exercise every day, believing that it will eventually bring the final positive result. And, indeed, it did. The healing was finally completed within a few months.

Today, after years of discipleship, I can say that the greatest self-healing is the healing performed on the consciousness. It is the balance that I found inside of me and the change in my relationship with people. These are the result of the knowledge I received from the Society, which help me in the task of self-healing, and, also, in the healing of other patients."

A different self-healing was the one Alexander per-
formed, another member of the healing section. It was
different because he used another regimen and because
the effect was immediate, as he said so himself:

"One day I sat down to perform my regular morning
meditation. I could not relax as I had a pain on the right
side of my head which was especially intense. Then the
words of the Master came to my mind: that the healer
heals with the hands but visualising them not as his or
her own, but as the hands of the Entity. I immediately put
these words into practice. I raised my hand and touched
the point where my head hurt, simply visualising it as
the hand of the Entity. I did not need to do anything else.
I felt a force penetrating me, acting on the area where I
felt the pain and completely dissolving it. In less than a
few seconds I was completely well."

The spiritual healers learn to recognise the Entity and
its curative power everywhere, as we have already men-
tioned. They learn to see all healings as spiritual healing
and to combine all methods, whenever there is need for
a better and more direct result. This is what John did
when he had tendonitis which was caused by exhaustive
work.

"I had a pain in my hand from tendonitis and, while
performing spiritual healing, I realised that I had to visit
a doctor. And so I did. The doctor gave me medication

and told me to be patient and not to tire my hand be-
cause such conditions cause great pain and are slow to
pass.

I immediately began taking the doctor's medication,
but, at the same time, I also performed spiritual heal-
ing. I decided that I had to quickly get well, combining
both treatments, because I had to return to my job soon.
Every time I performed self-healing the pain lessened sig-
nificantly. Thus, on the fourth day I was able to work
without difficulty. In one week I was completely well and
tendonitis never bothered me again. I believe that spir-
itual healing contributed to this, but, mostly, my faith
that all healing methods are the work of God."

Many more self-healings have been performed by spir-
itual healers. I will convey one of them here, because it
presents a peculiarity, it does not bring an immediate re-
sult, but in fact exhibits the symptom of fever, which can
contribute to the healing by "burning" the germs inside
the body. This self-healing was described by a spiritual
healer named Helen:

"I recently had a sinusitis attack. A closed nose and
throat, mucus, and pain. I sat down to perform a healing
on myself, and, after deeply relaxing, began my work.

I first visualised my nose within the light and I 'saw'
the light penetrating the sinuses and illuminating them.
Then I did the same for my throat, 'seeing' the light in-
ternally illuminating it again. While I worked, I visualised

the power of God flowing through my throat and sinuses and I repeated the Master's words, that the Entity heals the Entity, that the healer as well as the patient is the Entity.

As time passed, my nose stopped running, my throat cleared up and I felt relief. When I finished the self-healing I felt a great warmth and, after placing a thermometer, I saw that I had a fever (37.7°C). This would have surprised me, had I not known that the fever is a burning that accelerates the healing. And, indeed, it did. In two or three hours the fever had passed and I felt very well."

The healing that a healer performs on oneself greatly contributes to the expanding of the consciousness. As one unites with the spiritual field, one receives from it not only the power, but also the knowledge needed to find the cause of the disease. And this knowledge is often in itself a healing, as shown in the example given by a healer:

"One night, as I was returning home, I felt a strong pain in my calf. I walked as fast as I could to get home and meditate, to see what had happened and to work on the healing of the pain. Indeed, so I did, as soon as I reached my room. I calmed down, immersed into meditation and waited for the cause of my discomfort to be revealed. Some time passed and at one point the voice of my conscience gave me the answer I needed. And this came with a single word that sprang from my mind, the word 'Pity'.

At first I did not understand what pity had to do with the pain in my calf. Soon, however, my mind lit up and I started forming the correct thoughts, which led me to the discovery of the truth. That afternoon I had attended a place with some of my relatives, for whom I had felt pity, because they did not deal with spirituality as I did. I did not turn the various feelings of compassion that over-whelmed me into love, nor did I convey to them a stream of spirituality. I could not go above their emotional, self-ish functions, because I, too, functioned selfishly, con-sidering myself superior to them. My attitude created a retention of energy that accumulated in my calf causing this intense discomfort.

As soon as I realised my mistake, the pain started to subside and completely passed once I started bring-ing my relatives to mind and surrounding them in light, in the spiritual power. The retention left and I stood up thanking God for the knowledge given to me, in order to understand the problem and heal myself."

Is the power of the Spirit unlimited? Yes, it is, and this is proven daily to spiritual healers when they open themselves to it with faith and trust, recognising that the Spirit of God has a positive effect on everything, on the mind, on the emotions, on the body, on any material form. This is proven by a healing described by one of the Master's first disciples:

"One day I felt a pain in my right bunion, where I had an operation a few years ago. At the time, the bunion was removed and an artificial component had been put in its place. The doctor that had performed the surgery had told me that these components have a limited life span and that in a few years I would have to undergo a second surgery, in order to replace it with a new one. When I felt the pain in my bunion, which had not bothered me all these years, I considered performing self-healing. As I immersed myself in meditation, I 'saw' that there was no problem with my foot, but the problem was with the component. I remembered the doctor's words and stopped the healing work, considering that it would have no effect, because my foot was well and the only thing 'ill' was a human construct. I stood up and the pain continued.

The next day I mentioned the matter to the Master, saying that it was likely that I would soon have to be operated on again. The answer he gave me left me dumbfounded, I had never expected to hear what he said:

'The power of the Spirit intervenes in everything, in the entire natural world. Why cannot it intervene on this component, too? Perform the healing with the belief that the problem will be eliminated if it is God's will.'

That same day I did as the Master told me. I delved into meditation and let the flow of spiritual power descend to my foot and penetrate the artificial component, visualising that everything can possibly happen, because everything is God's work. In a few minutes the pain started to leave and half an hour later it had completely disappeared. Three years have passed since this healing and my bunion is completely well.

The doctor that had operated on me, and whom a friend of mine went to visit for a problem of her own, was interested to know how I was, wondering why I still had not gone to change the old component. When he was informed that I was completely well he was startled for a moment but then said: 'You see, then, that everything is in our mind.' His words intersect with the Society's teaching that says that health and disease are affected by the human's mental state and that the potential for exercising spiritual healing is within everyone, as long as they have their mind and heart open to the healing power of God."

Self-healing and healing on other patients are essentially the same thing, they are a healing towards a certain weak field and so they should be dealt with by every spiritual healer. The Society's healers are trained in this. They learn to have the same attitude towards their personal problems as well as towards the problems of others; to consider all beings part of the Entity which heals all of its aspects. Regarding this issue, one of the most senior spiritual healers says the following:

"I thank God who helps me to work as a spiritual healer. I thank Him for gradually leading me to the awareness of the pure spiritual field. To this field I uplift all healings and self-healings that I perform. I place there all retentions present in the patient's energy body and I visualise that they are dissolved and that health returns. I work for others and for myself, leaving the outcome of the work to be done according to the will of God."

EDITOR'S NOTE

As was also mentioned in the prologue, Mrs Kiki Keramida passed away before the completion of her book. The previous chapters were written by her and were submitted to Mrs Klairi, just before her passing. The following chapters have been written by Mrs Klairi, with the combined effort of the spiritual healers that had worked with Mrs Kiki as members of the Society's healing section, the responsibility of which she had undertaken at the time.

In the following pages, the importance of Mrs Kiki's contribution will be shown, not only for her work as a healer, but also for the foundations she laid concerning the healing section's organisation. The fact that her attitude towards the other healers was a brace for them, an assistance in their spiritual course, will also be shown. She was the living example of a disciple that systematically worked to overcome her personal problems, always willing to selflessly offer her services whenever she could.

The organisation and monitoring of a healing section is no simple task. On the contrary, it is a complex and multifaceted effort. It requires supervision on multiple fields and constant vigilance in order to avoid errors. Monitoring the patients' progress is not enough, it is also necessary to possess the knowledge concerning the method of their healing, as well as the correct way to approach them. Simply training the healers is not sufficient; an interest in their problems and evolution is also required. In other words, what is needed is faith and devotion to the calling, something that Mrs Kiki steadily showed throughout the years that she worked as head of the Servers Society's healing section.

THE ORGANISATION OF THE HEALING SECTION

At the time when Mrs Kiki undertook the task of organising the healing section, it was necessary for her to deal with two different areas. One was all the practical work that had to be done regularly by herself and the rest of the healers. The other, which was also the hardest, involved everything having to do with the human factor, in other words with her contact with the patients but also with the healers themselves, most of whom were still in their early stages of training.

The practical issues were soon put into a fairly satisfactory order. The "distant" and "contact" healing sections were established and later on a section for visiting patients, too. At the same time certain forms were standardised, informing the patients of their obligations, which were very simple. They had to send the medical data regarding their illness and regularly inform the healing section on the course of their health. The patients had no financial obligation to the Society as spiritual healing is always performed selflessly. The groups of healers were also organised, and each one, with the guidance of a proven healer, undertook the healing of a certain number of patients. A meeting day for all healers was also appointed for their comprehensive briefing and training. The assembly of the spiritual healing section was soon completed, based on all the relevant data that already existed, and the work on its implementation started immediately.

A problem that came up was the same which Mrs Kiki had already mentioned, namely the difficulty in communication with the patients, which persisted despite the section's organisation. The patients, as is only natural, have many mood swings. They are excited with the idea that spiritual healing will immediately cure them but then they are disappointed when that does not happen. If, on the other hand, they get well, they might ignore the help they received from the healing section and discontinue their contact with it, without ever explaining why. They often neglect to inform or, contrarily, constantly call the healers for the slightest issue that appears. The same is done by those acting on behalf of a patient, when he or she is underage or unable to communicate. The healers understand the difficulties of these patients that are caused by their fears, doubts and agony concerning their health. They also know that it is not easy explaining to them about the work of spiritual healing and the importance of their proper and regular informing on the progress of their condition. I believe this problem will always exist to a certain degree, as experience has taught us so. At the beginning of the healing section's organisation this problem was more intensified due to the immaturity of the healers who created emotional relationships with their patients. Sometimes they wanted to continue the healing on patients that did not regularly update, sometimes they got tired of the multitude of phone calls they received and other times they were disappointed when a patient discontinued his or her association with spiritual healing. Mrs Kiki had to supervise all these reactions of the novice healers and constantly talk to them and help them function in a more detached way. She communicated with the patients herself, and, at the same time, undertook the task of collecting all of their updates and doing the work that the other healers were not yet in a position to do.

Regarding this issue, a healer says the following: "Mrs Kiki constantly spurred us to become responsible and immediate in the needs that were presented both with patients and with the practical work. As we did not yet have the alertness we needed and were often lured by our emotions and personal problems, she undertook the work that we had to do, showing patience and acceptance for the difficulties we presented."

Mrs Kiki's experiences from the period of her initial training with all the doubts and misgivings she had at the time proved very useful. She knew how to help the new healers and set an example to them with her presence and actions. A healer says:

"What helped me to consolidate myself as a healer was Mrs Kiki's stance, a spiritual healer's stance, responding immediately to whatever was presented. I had the good fortune to work with her on a 'contact' healing and to see on a practical level the simplicity and tranquillity during the healing. With her guidance I learned to delve into the patients' problem, to 'hear' and 'see' internally, so as to understand in what way to help them."

The Master has always stressed the importance of the knowledge that should be received by members of the Society regarding issues of science, philosophy, society etc. These include some key elements of the human body, which especially help those wanting to become spiritual healers. In the booklets taught at the Society there are medical texts on the organs of the human body as well as on certain diseases. Following the instructions of the Master, Mrs Kiki organised the healing section's library and supplied it with a modern medical encyclopaedia and other related books. Her goal was for the healers to understand that alongside their internal meditative work, a certain knowledge was also necessary. To stimulate their interest, she often gave them according projects, as a healer says:

"Mrs Kiki instructed us to perform specific studies on the organs of the human body. These projects aided us on focusing during the healings and to also observe the conditions and problems appearing on our own body. She taught us to take care of our health, to listen to the doctors and to follow the dictates of medical science. Many projects were completed thanks to her efforts and were later studied by all the members of the healing section."

The reader possibly believes it is obvious that healers should study the human body, since they work on aiding its cure. My personal experience has shown that a novice healer does not always have this interest. As they are in the early stages of meditation, they are more preoccupied with the experiences they receive by becoming aware of the flow of energies through the body or understanding certain deeper causes of diseases. The study of medical issues does not offer them this new element which they consider "magical", and for this reason are not as willing to deal with their studies. The composition of meditative experiences and specific knowledge comes gradually, as the healer passes more and more into the state of offering and no longer cares about the satisfaction received with the revelations made at the time of the healing. Mrs Kiki knew all of this and that is why she always insisted on projects about the human body to which she gradually added the studies about the energy body and its connection to the organism.

Alongside this work, something that healers should never neglect is their individual spiritual course. This is the basis of their healing work and that is why they all regularly attend the "self-study" groups and work under the guidance of specially trained group leaders. As head of the healing section, Mrs Kiki often had to discuss with the healers and many times, during the conversation, personal issues arose, which had to be addressed by her if they affected the functioning of the healers in their healing work. Depending on the case, she conveyed to them the elements she had received from the Master, as seen in the following examples. A healer says:

"Mrs Kiki was strict and absolute when circumstances required it, particularly concerning the relations between the healers as well as those between them and their patients. Many times she would say to me: 'What you said was not right. You lack discretion. Put yourself in the other's place and you will see your own error.'"

A healer gives a different view from her contact with Mrs Kiki, who always mentally encouraged her, in order to reduce her constant tendency for self-criticism that did not let her express what she felt: "The great lesson I learned from Mrs Kiki, in a way I did not even realise, was that I could easily open up to her and was not afraid to talk to her; I was not embarrassed to tell her about what was happening to me. This resulted in my beginning to open up within myself, without shame, without guilt, and to see things that I would not have dared to see previously. That is how I learned to accept myself, and, also, to understand and accept others."

Another member of the Society says the following: "At the beginning of my discipleship, despite my deep intuition that it was a positive thing to be close to the Master, whom I had searched for unconsciously, I also I had many doubts at the same time. When I conveyed them to Mrs Kiki, she told me that she once had doubts, too, but they soon dispelled. Mrs Kiki became a kind of bridge that connected me to the Master, as she always gave me warmth. I felt secure seeing her kindness, her modesty, but also her healing ability, that had often helped me, too, whenever I needed it."

Many times Mrs Kiki performed healing on members of the Society and this was often an incentive for them to decide to also become healers, as a healer says:

"When I came to the Society I had colitis and a lump in my right breast, which could possibly develop into cancer. Mrs Kiki performed a 'contact' healing on me and soon the colitis passed and the lump disappeared. What impressed me every time I had a healing was the love I experienced and I understood that it was the love of God, conveyed by Mrs Kiki, because of her interest for me. This love made me decide to become a spiritual healer myself, to learn to love the human. Something else that I learned from these healings was that the healer must have stability and consistency towards the responsibility he or she has assumed."

The consistency and faith of Mrs Kiki is also mentioned by another member of the healing section: "Mrs Kiki's home was close to mine and so for almost a whole year we returned from the Society with my car. This drive was always a learning process for me. Her words, her faith in the Society's spiritual work, in the Master and in spiritual healing reinforced and encouraged me constantly in the course of my discipleship."

I mentioned all these examples and opinions of healers to mainly illustrate one element, that the healing work is the work of the soul. It does not rely only on specific knowledge or the handling of practical work, as it does not rely on the hours spent by the individuals at the patients' healings. It is based on the healer's spiritual function that guides them to the mergence with all that they are called to do and learn, in a theoretical, practical and meditative level. The mergence, as the Master says, is what simplifies everything that seems complicated, it brings the immediacy in the response to the needs, thus accomplishing the healing work. This message was what Mrs Kiki tried to convey to the healers, setting an example with her own stance, the stance of the disciple continuously trained while providing service to others.

VISITS TO PATIENTS

With the Society's founding, and before the training of disciples in spiritual healing had begun, the only one who performed healings was the Master. This was usually performed at the Society's site on people who came to meet us while having certain health problems. Sometimes the Master also visited patients who had been informed of his healing work and wished to receive his aid. Usually, one of his disciples also accompanied him on these visits, so that he or she acquired knowledge and experiences on the functioning of the healer. When the three most senior disciples formed the first healing group, the healings were only performed at the Society, so that the healers could consult the Master whenever they needed to. Later, they too began visiting patients at their homes or at the hospital if they had requested it and were unable to come to the Society.

At the time when Mrs Kiki took over the healing section, particular attention had been paid to the training of the new healers and the organisation of the section in general. The most senior healers had many other responsibilities that left them very little free time for visits to patients, except on rare occasions. The novice healers were not yet sufficiently established in the practice of spiritual healing so as to work outside the Society. Thus, this section barely functioned, as other more immediate needs came first. With Mrs Kiki's presence at the healing section, and after many organisational issues were settled, the need for regular visits to patients arose again. This was, of course, natural, as the number of patients constantly grew and among them certain that were bedridden. That is when Mrs Kiki requested from the healers that had received the necessary training by now, to state if they were able to also undertake visits to patients. Her purpose was to create a group that would carry out this particular task. Soon, four members of the healing section responded to her request and stated that they were especially interested in this line of work. Despite their interest, they still had certain reservations, as a member of that group notes:

"We knew that some patients were in great need of 'contact' healing and that they were unable to come to the Society, because their illness confined them to a bed or a wheelchair. We wanted to visit them, but in the beginning we were somewhat hesitant. The nature of the task we were called to do troubled us. What would we face in an environment unknown to us? How would the patients' relatives treat us? Would there be suitable conditions for us to perform the healing? And above all, how would we deal with any potential problems that arose during a healing?

Following Mrs Kiki's advice, we mentioned all of these concerns to the Master, seeking his opinion. He immediately urged us to respond to this need saying that we were experienced enough to cope with this task. He also said that we should not be concerned with the difficulties we would be facing, because we knew how to deal with them. In accordance with the Master's advice, we began the first 'contact' healings on the patients we visited. The guidance of the group was in the hands of the most experienced healer. We did not encounter any particular problems, as the patients and their relatives accepted us with great pleasure. We explained the method of healing, if they had not previously experienced it, and emphasised the need for peace and calm during our time of work. They were very understanding of what we told them. We soon realised that we indeed had the ability to work as healers outside the Society's site, as the Master had assured us."

With the establishment of this group regular healings began on patients incapable of coming to the Society. The healers visited them sometimes at their homes and other times at the clinics or hospitals were they were treated. Depending on the case, the healing could continue for some time or could be promptly completed, as indeed, also happened with the healings performed at the Society. The following healing examples have been given by members of that group.

"One day the husband of a multiple sclerosis patient came to the Society, asking for the aid of spiritual healing. The disease was in a very advanced stage and as a result the patient was completely incapable of walking for the last nine months, being able to move only with the use of a wheelchair. Under these circumstances we decided to visit her at home, something that pleased her husband greatly. When we met the patient the following day, we were astonished by her tranquillity and attitude towards her problem. She said she believed that her illness was given to her in order to make her change internally and deal with spiritual matters. This attitude considerably helped in the healing we performed on her. She was so merged with the healing current that, after the end of the healing, she felt strong enough to get up from the wheelchair and take a few steps entirely on her own. The healing continued for several months and the results were very positive. She could walk, with difficulty, of course, inside her house and do some simple chores. In the end she was well enough to come to the Society accompanied by her husband, so that we could perform her healing there."

Another case of a healing performed at the patient's home is the one described by one more member of that group:

"One day we went to the home of a patient with a severe form of cancer that had spread throughout his entire body. The doctors did not give him much time and they could only aid in relieving his suffering as much possible. We had previously performed 'distant' healing on this patient at the Society, but with his condition deteriorating, we had started going to his home, too.

When we arrived at his home that day, his daughter greeted us with great relief. Her fatigue and anxiety, as she dealt on a daily basis with her father's illness, could clearly be seen on her face. She led us to the patient's room and then left, letting us perform the healing.

As soon as the patient saw us, he seemed to take courage, getting out of bed on his own and sitting in an armchair. At first we talked to him a bit, and he told us that he was in great pain, but that every time we performed a healing on him, the pain decreased. He also said that he had calmed down and had stopped worrying about the future of his family, as he usually did. After the discussion we began the healing. The patient had closed his eyes, relinquishing himself to the healing current, while his face had taken on a serene expression. When we finished, we asked him how he felt and he replied that he felt stronger and that the pain had softened considerably. He thanked us and asked us to perform 'remote' healing on him as well as also visiting him more often.

After the healing we went into the living room, where we sat and chatted with his daughter, who also seemed to be in need of healing, as the state she was living in had been very tiring to her. She thanked us for our concern and the time we devoted on healing her father.

A month later we were informed that this patient had passed away and that his death was very calm, without the suffering normally experienced by patients with this type of cancer. His daughter sent us a thank-you letter, in which she wrote that she believed the way in which her father died was due to the help he had received from spiritual healing."

Naturally, the healers that visited patients dealt with very serious cases and often the work they did was more palliative than curative. The patients calmed down, their pains decreased, their mood improved, but the advanced state of their disease rarely allowed for a complete healing. Other times, they faced the denial of the patients, who, despite asking for their help, did not go on to accept it, for reasons that have been mentioned previously by Mrs Kiki. I, too, had such an experience, even before the group that visited the patients was organised. I remember visiting a patient with paralysis of the lower limbs, who had asked us to perform a "contact" healing on him. When I went to his house and even after talking extensively about the Society and spiritual healing with him, in the end he stated that he wished to tackle the problem solely on his own powers without the help of anyone else. He gave no other explanation for his denial, nor did we ever learn about the progress of his health.

Another patient, who had a completely different attitude, called me to come to the clinic one day before his scheduled prostate surgery. As soon as he saw me, he asked his relatives to leave us alone for a while and prepared for the healing, calming and experiencing the serenity and power passing into his body. The next day, he underwent surgery as planned, and it went very well. What impressed the doctors was the patient's minimal postoperative pains and his very quick recovery. He attributed this positive course to the spiritual healing he had received the day before his surgery.

The group that had been established to make visits to patients worked systematically for two years. During this time many healings took place, which exhibited a similar course to those performed at the Society. The only difference was the psychological support of the patients who in this way felt the immediate concern of the healers and trusted them more, as they appreciated the time spent to visit them. At the end of the second year the group discontinued its regular visits as the many family and other obligations of its members did not leave them enough time to continue. A key benefit of this work, apart from the aid received by certain patients, was the healers' establishment in their healing work. The fact that they had worked on their own, away from the Society, having the ability to handle all the difficulties that arose, validated to them the power of spiritual healing. Today they all work as proven healers within the groups functioning in the Society.

Visits to patients' homes now happen very rarely and only in emergencies. Perhaps in the future, if the need arises, a new group might be created to take on this task. What has been validated to the healers, especially the senior ones, is that the effects of spiritual healing are not affected by distance. The energy transferred from the healer to the patient acts alike on the problem whether it is a "contact" or "distant" healing that is performed. This has been proven many times by patients who, without knowing when spiritual healing is being performed on them, can identify the time of the healers' work, because they can feel at that time certain positive changes in their bodies and in their mental attitude.

The patients, however, do not always have the adequate sensitivity in order to feel the current of spiritual healing. As the Master says, the patients are in need of a certain presence, they want to see the healers next to them, to rely on them, to see the work performed through their hands. That is why there is a "contact" healing section at the Society. That is the reason why the healers, who are aware of this need that the patients have, do not rule out visits to homes or clinics and hospitals, whenever, of course, it is deemed necessary and accomplishable. The example has been given by the Master himself, who, as I mentioned at the beginning of the chapter, made visits to patients who requested it. Responding to this need, Mrs Kiki organised the group of healers, whose experience from visits to patients has helped the whole healing section and has laid the foundations for the continuation of their work.

ILLNESS AND DEATH

Something that might have surprised the reader of this book is that Mrs Kiki refers to her illness only in her first chapters. This omission might have created the impression that the author was completely well up to the time when the cancer metastasised to her bones. There were indeed large intervals during which she felt as if she had never been sick or had undergone any surgery. There were, however, periods when her health troubled her greatly. At certain times her arm on the side of her mastectomy swelled up considerably and she ran a high fever. At other times, she experienced pain in various parts of her body, which she dealt with the help of spiritual healing as well as classical medicine. Approximately five years before her passing away, her second breast, which had a malignant tumour, was also removed. Her situation deteriorated considerably over the next two years, with the emergence of aggravations in her bones.

During the fifteen years that Mrs Kiki was at the Society, she never neglected her work as a healer. This was something she did not only when she was well, but even when she had a problem, too. As was only natural, the state of her health upset her during those times. She performed self-healing, the other healers as well as the Master performed spiritual healings on her, but she quickly forgot all this as soon as her troubles passed.

The Master often noted to her that she should take greater care of her health, without ignoring her body by showing excessive responsiveness to any need that arose, and to limit her dealings with the healing section's practical tasks. He also told her to regularly visit her doctors and perform spiritual healing on herself on a daily basis. She followed his advice, but she was more concerned with the issues of the healing section, its organisation, its patients and its healers. This I believe to be the reason for which she barely mentions her illness in the chapters of her book. Her problem became non-existent to her whenever she had another issue to deal with, as in this case, conveying her experiences as a spiritual healer to the reader.

Regarding her attitude towards her illness, a healer that had known her for many years, says the following:

"Mrs Kiki, up to the last moment, never saw her personal problem as an obstacle in the work she had chosen to do. I was moved many times by her function, but I was also motivated to improve my position as a healer. It was remarkable to see how simply she talked of her illness and how easily she sidestepped it whenever someone else's problem called her to perform spiritual healing."

Another, novice healer that had not been informed of Mrs Kiki's illness, expressed great surprise upon realising the problem:

"I was overwhelmed, when, without knowing that Mrs Kiki was sick, accidentally touched her swollen hand. I could not imagine how a person could offer so much to patients and healers, when she was ill herself. And to do so without raising suspicions, as her offering was always so immediate."

Mrs Kiki's attitude remained the same even when her health had deteriorated so much that she could no longer come to the Society. She often called to those that had replaced her at the healing section and requested information about the patients, to whom she continued to perform healings from her home. Her concern for others was expressed in many ways. If a healer called her asking about her health, she briefly responded and proceeded to ask him or her about the healing section. When one of the Master's disciples visited her, her main interest was anything regarding the Society's course. Whenever I went to her house, our main discussion topic was the book she was writing along with everything else she wanted to write and expand on.

An impressive affirmation of her interest for others was what she told me when I visited her for the last time. In those days she was being hospitalised, as she was in need of a blood transfusion. She was under the influence of powerful medications that kept her sedated at most times, keeping the pains at bay. She would only come to and communicate with her environment for moments at a time. At such a moment, as I sat next to her, she opened her eyes, looked at me and said: "My thoughts, Klairi, are of all those who are sick and in need of medical care but have no medical insurance. How will they be able to cover their expenses?" I did not have time to recover from the surprise her words caused me, when she descended again, without giving me a chance to respond. I saw, however, once again, that despite her illness, she was still concerned with the problems of others.

Perhaps the question arises of why healers cannot heal themselves with self-healing, why cannot the spiritual healing of other healers or medical science heal them. The Master has already answered this question in the words often conveyed by Mrs Kiki in her book: "Only God's will can decide if a patient should be healed or not." To humans death often seems unfair, especially if the person dying has the potential to perform charitable work. Humans, however, see things in their own way, judge them in their own logic and deal with them in their own emotions. A person's life cycle ends when it must end, when the person's soul completes its work. And the time for this to happen is something no one can judge, except for the Entity itself. This teaching has been given by the Master to all healers and members of the Society. It states that humans must always take care of their health and do their duty towards their bodies; they are explicitly forbidden from ending their lives, but must calmly accept this ending when it comes from God.

The chapter that Mrs Kiki wanted to write while she was still well, was a chapter about death. As she had mentioned to me, she was at the time gathering certain data concerning cases of patients that had passed away after having received the aid of spiritual healing. According to the information from relatives that had contacted the healing section after the death of these patients, the way in which they died was very calm. It is a fact that spiritual healing always helps, even in the last moments before death. This chapter was never written, but proof, however, of all those that Mrs Kiki wanted to write was her own death. The healing she constantly performed on everyone had helped her in her own spiritual course, in the attitude with which she faced life and, also, death.

We cannot know what the course of Mrs Kiki's health would have been, had she not come to the Society and become a healer. What I believe, from my personal experience as a healer, is that she was greatly helped from the practice of spiritual healing that always rejuvenates the healer's body. This is what she, too, advocated, proving it with the strength to work so hard, despite her problem. She also noted that she immediately dealt with many of her symptoms by self-healing. Besides all this, I believe that what mainly helped her was the teaching she received from the Master and the example he set himself with his attitude towards the health problems he had been dealing with since an early age.

At the time when Mrs Kiki stopped coming to the Society due to her health problems, the Master was already gravely ill, passing away a few months later. One day, despite his considerable suffering, he was informed that Mrs Kiki was feeling ill and was in pain, and he was saddened by her condition. Ignoring his own problems, the Master took care to send one of his disciples to her home and drive her back to his home. He then proceeded to have a lengthy conversation with her, a lesson that revitalised her mentally, as ascertained by the disciples that saw her after the end of the lesson.

I did not personally attend this lesson, so I am not

in a position to know exactly what the Master said to Mrs Kiki. What I understood, however, from a meeting I had with her the next day, was that his interest for her, at a time when he was so in such a poor state, gave her exactly what she needed. He gave her assurance, love, and provided a living example of what selflessness and contribution means. He gave her one more confirmation of what she mentions herself at the beginning of her book, that the Master was himself the spiritual principles which he taught. These principles are taught to all disciples and they work on applying them in their lives. This is the work Mrs Kiki did, too, as evidenced by the work she offered as a healer and as head of the Society's healing section.

EPILOGUE

As an epilogue to Mrs Kiki Keramida, we cite opinions of spiritual healers who worked with her for many years, while she was in charge of the healing section.

"Mrs Kiki gave me love and showed me the importance of the immediate, practical interest. She showed me how to have a firm position as a disciple and as a spiritual healer. She would aid you whenever you asked for her help, no matter what."

"Mrs Kiki's aim was the perfection of herself through her constant discipleship and the conveyance of her knowledge to the novice disciples. I am grateful for all that she gave me."

"Mrs Kiki helped me to see with detachment the results of spiritual healing. That is how I learned to slowly accept every result and trust in God's will; to not forget that behind the negative aspect of illness is the positive one that is related to the course and evolution of the soul."

"At the lessons she taught to the groups, Mrs Kiki was especially cooperative with the other disciples. She believed in their powers and, following the Master's instructions, always tried to make those powers come out of the hearts and minds of the healers."

"Mrs Kiki helped patients realise that spiritual healing is something simple and that every person has the ability to discover its strength inside of him or her and express it. She also told them that any healer, including herself, can be found in the patient's position. Her words helped me to see spiritual healing simply, as a way of life, and to work without intensity and effort."

"In the personal conversations with the disciples, Mrs Kiki urged them to find their own solutions to their problems. She gave them, whenever needed, the clues that would help them understand the causes of any problem and work on them. She effectively implemented the methods of communication and dialogue that she had been taught by the Master."

Much more has been written by the spiritual healers about Mrs Kiki. They all express their appreciation for her work and her great responsiveness to any need. Conclud-

ing this epilogue, we convey the words of a healer that show the importance of spiritual work, when practiced with faith and devotion:

"What remains and what ultimately matters is that, through all Mrs Kiki has bequeathed to us with her work and her example, one thing will never happen: she will never cease to be in our hearts!"

Kiki Keramida

The author was born in 1929 in Volos, Greece, where she spent her childhood and adolescence and where she married in 1958. One year later, she and her husband moved to Athens where they had a daughter. She passed away at the beginning of 1997.

Her interest in the human ability to have a positive influence on the state of one's health had begun in 1972. At that time, she herself had faced a serious health problem. In 1982 she became acquainted with Omilos Eksipiretiton (The Servers' Society) Spiritual Centre and its founder, philosopher and writer Master Dimitris Kakalidis. Since then she followed the teaching of the Society and was trained in spiritual healing. Later on, she assumed responsibility for the organisation and supervision of the Spiritual Healing section of the Society.

See also...

ઉ૪

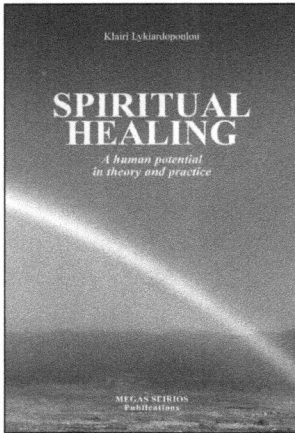

"Spiritual Healing – A human potential in theory and practice" by Klairi Lykiardopoulou

"People have the potential to heal themselves and others", says the author of this book. The idea is a startling one, yet it brings us an optimistic message. Klairi Lykiardopoulou goes on to explain that this potential exists because the Power of the Spirit exists in all of us. The author gives many examples that prove that Spiritual Healing is a reality. The book ends with the author's optimistic vision: "The day will soon come when all healing methods will work together for a single aim: to help people to become healthier and happier!"

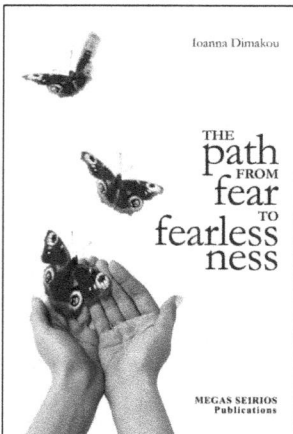

"The Path from Fear to Fearlessness" by Ioanna Dimakou

In a simple and clear language, the author describes her efforts to "conquer" fear, which for three years were a daily problem in her life. This problem was greatly reduced within the first five months after the day she met Dimitris Kakalidis and received his help. It is an example that may help those who experience similar fears and phobias. The positive results she experienced led her to seek the path of spirituality and continue her progress to fearlessness.

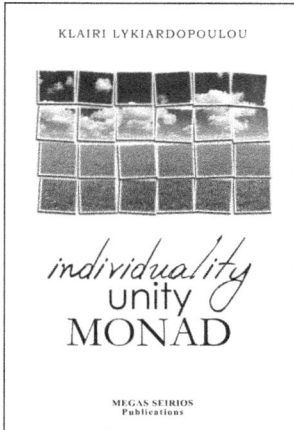

"Individuality - Unity - Monad"
by Klairi Lykiardopoulou

KLAIRI LYKIARDOPOULOU

individuality
unity &
MONAD

MEGAS SEIRIOS
Publications

This book speaks of the spiritual progress of man from the unconscious to the conscious, from the individual to the Monad. It describes the processes through which the human being passes from the moment he becomes aware of his individuality. He then expresses two desires, one to preserve his individuality, and the other to become a member of a group. And by participating in other groups, he realises at some point that his nature is like that of all men...

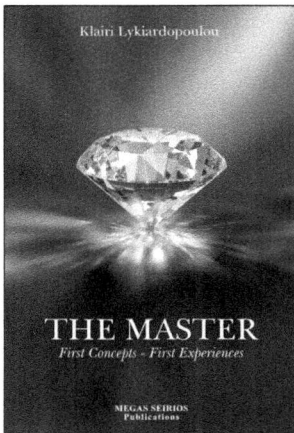

"The Master
– First Concepts - First Experiences"
by Klairi Lykiardopoulou

Klairi Lykiardopoulou

THE MASTER
First Concepts - First Experiences

MEGAS SEIRIOS
Publications

In this first volume of the series The Master the author speaks of her experiences as a result of her meeting the Master, Dimitris Kakalidis. She describes how he responded in such a way as to help her understand concepts that were unknown to her. She wanted to follow his teaching because she could see the spirituality that he transmitted to all his disciples...

MEGAS SEIRIOS PUBLICATIONS
English Editions

The Concealed Lotus of Manifestation
Fallen Paradise Holy Matter
Logos the Third
a poetic trilogy by Dimitris Kakalidis (bilingual edition)

Incentives I & Incentives II
poetic collections by Dimitris Kakalidis (bilingual edition)

The Revelation of the Entity
by Dimitris Kakalidis

The Wisdom of the Poem
by Dimitris Kakalidis

Spiritual Healing,
A human potential in theory and practice
by Klairi Lykiardopoulou

The Master [1],
First Concepts – First Experiences
by Klairi Lykiardopoulou

The Path from Fear to Fearlessness
by Ioanna Dimakou

Individuality Unity Monad
by Klairi Lykiardopoulou

Seeking... from Alpha to Omega,
Synthesis of Science and Philosophy
by Mina Gouvatsou-Karekou

I Will be Here (poetry)
by Paraskevi Kostopetrou

• **Small Temples on a Wave** (poetry)
• **Fiery Notion** (poetry)
by Vassiliki Ergazaki

Experiences of a Spiritual Healer
by Kiki Keramida

...And the Shadows Became Light
by Klairi Lykiardopoulou

You can Open Your Eyes Now
by Ade Durojaiye

Greek Editions

Dimitris Kakalidis
- The Wisdom of the Poem
- The Wisdom of the Short Story

Poetic Trilogy:
- The Hidden Lotus of Revelation
- Fallen Paradise Holy Matter
- Logos the Third

Poetic Collection:
- Incentives I
- Incentives II

- The Revelation of the Entity

Klairi Lykiardopoulou
- Woman - Exploring her Position and Role in Society
- Man - Exploring his Position and Role in Society
- Couple - Exploring its Position and Role in Society
- Spiritual Healing, *A human potential in theory and practice*
- The Master [1], *First Concepts – First Experiences*
- The Master [2], *The Awakening of the Soul*
- The Master [3], *Processes of the Mind*
- The Master [4], *Accomplishment – Spiritual Healing*
- The Knowledge of the Educator
- The Power of the Woman
- Man and Money, *A philosophical study of their relationship*
- Individuality Unity Monad
- The Family Circle
- The Sacred Task of the Soul
- The Heart of the Earth, *Imaginary Short-stories to give Light to our Planet!*
- The Diachronic Master [1], *Seeking the Knowledge in simple thoughts and deeds*
- The Diachronic Master [2], *Discipleship in the Eternal Truths*
- The Diachronic Master [3], *The Power of Love*
- The Diachronic Master [4], *Our Hidden and Apparent Self*
- ... And the Shadows became Light

Dimitris Karvounis – Dimitris Kakalidis
Alalum and Hallelujah (poetry)

Dimitris Karvounis
- The Crypt and the Nest (and other stories)
- Lilian
- My Spirit Crucified (poetry)
- The Eternally Collected (poetry)

Ninon Dimitriadou-Kampouri
Fear Not, Day is Breaking! (poetry)

Ioanna Dimakou
The Path from Fear to Fearlessness

Kiki Keramida
Experiences of a Spiritual Healer

Petros Panteloglou
The Road I Chose
A Professional Driver's Path to Spirituality

Mina Gouvatsou-Karekou
Seeking... from Alpha to Omega
A Synthesis of Science and Philosophy

Vassiliki K. Ergazaki
- Small Temples on a Wave (poetry)
- Fiery Notion (poetry)
- For the Flowers to Sing (poetry)

Dionisis Dimakos
Flows of Reflection and Heart (poetry)

Paraskevi Kostopetrou
I Will be Here (poetry)

Ade Durojaiye
You Can Open Your Eyes Now